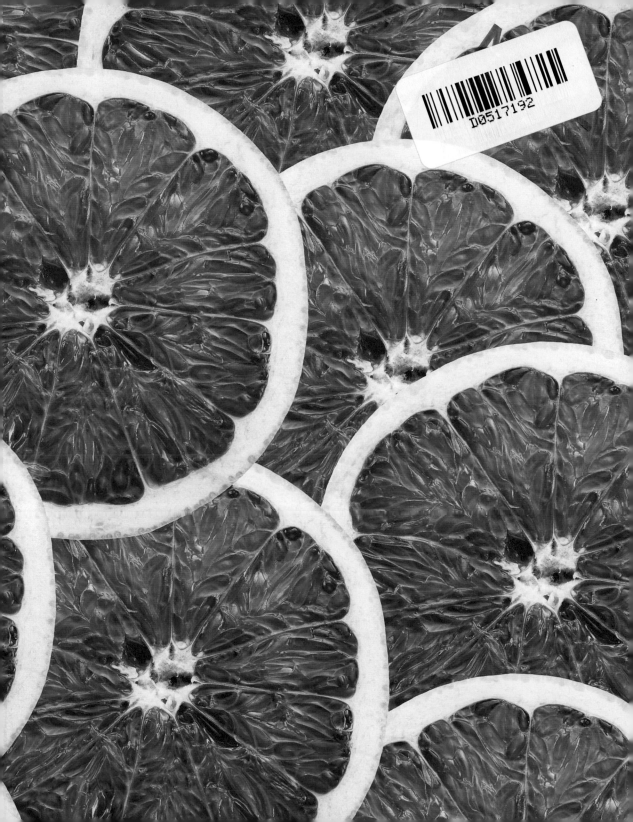

THE **HISTORY**

OF

FOOD

IN

101 OBJECTS

Media Lab Books
For inquiries, call 646-838-6637

Copyright 2017 Topix Media Lab

Published by Topix Media Lab
14 Wall Street, Suite 4B, New York, NY 10005

Printed in China

ISBN-10: 1-942556-65-9
ISBN-13: 978-1-942556-65-7

CEO **Tony Romando**

VICE PRESIDENT OF BRAND MARKETING **Joy Bomba**
DIRECTOR OF FINANCE **Vandana Patel**
DIRECTOR OF SALES AND NEW MARKETS **Tom Mifsud**
MANUFACTURING DIRECTOR **Nancy Puskuldjian**
FINANCIAL ANALYST **Matthew Quinn**
BRAND MARKETING ASSISTANT **Taylor Hamilton**

EDITOR-IN-CHIEF **Jeff Ashworth**
CREATIVE DIRECTOR **Steven Charny**
PHOTO DIRECTOR **Dave Weiss**
MANAGING EDITOR **Courtney Kerrigan**
SENIOR EDITORS **Tim Baker, James Ellis**

CONTENT EDITOR **Trevor Courneen**
CONTENT DESIGNER **Michelle Lock**
CONTENT PHOTO EDITOR **Catherine Armanasco**
ART DIRECTOR **Susan Dazzo**
ASSOCIATE ART DIRECTOR **Rebecca Stone**
ASSISTANT MANAGING EDITOR **Holland Baker**
DESIGNER **Danielle Santucci**
ASSISTANT PHOTO EDITOR **Jessica Ariel Wendroff**
ASSISTANT EDITORS **Alicia Kort, Kaytie Norman**
EDITORIAL ASSISTANT **Isabella Torchia**

CO-FOUNDERS **Bob Lee, Tony Romando**

"People who love to eat are always the best people."

—Julia Child

**T**HROUGHOUT its rich, ever-evolving and supersaturated history, food has been a mirror to society. In his gastronomy manifesto *The Physiology of Taste* (1825), French politician-turned-epicure Jean Anthelme Brillat-Savarin wrote, "Tell me what you eat and I will tell you what you are," a phrase that would plant the seed for the modern idiom, "You are what you eat." While most people today would probably prefer not to be defined by everything they eat—particularly on those "cheat days" where they polish off a pepperoni pizza and a pint of ice cream—that notion continues to carry weight (or at least explain weight gain). In the following pages, we explore the story of food's role in human history through 101 objects representing everything from agricultural revolutions to noncore convenience. And those who struggle to look into a can of SPAM and see their own reflection can take solace knowing that food, like humanity, often goes through phases.

TABLE OF CONTENTS

Laying the Food Foundation

In the earliest eras of civilization, humans discovered ways to cultivate their resources to create reliable food sources. The process yielded the foundation of modern agricultural and culinary practices.

FIRE

ABOUT 1.5 MILLION years ago, a cooking revolution was ignited when humans first put food to flame. While the first instance may have been as simple as a person tossing (or maybe even accidentally dropping) the limb of a fresh kill in an open fire, it would change the trajectory of food forever.

Fire became an essential feature in the human home by the Paleolithic era, roughly 200,000 to 40,000 years ago. Hearths were made with stones arranged in circles at the center of every home, providing both a source of warmth and a means of cooking. This would continue for many millennia until the 19th century when gas ranges became increasingly common components in homes.

The far more flavorful result of cooking over a fire—not to mention its prevention of foodborne illness—would be one humankind would never turn away from.

NUTTING STONE

WHILE DIGGING the area's first well in 1608, colonists in Jamestown, Virginia, discovered a sandstone block with a shallow depression.

Known to Virginian Native Americans as a *tockahoe*, the nutting stone was primarily used to prepare harvested nuts. Gatherers would place the nuts in the depression of the stone and then crack them open with another object, typically a wooden hammer or another stone. Pecans, walnuts and acorns were common, and the Native Americans of Virginia would also mash hickory nuts on the stone to produce a sweet, milky beverage.

As nutting stones evolved into nutcrackers over the course of several centuries, they became far more efficient. One even became an iconic ballet character.

3

THE SEED

YOU MAY BE QUICK to spit out the seeds when you eat an apple today, but in 19th-century America there was a serious need for seed. So much so, in the 1850s, the government had strict control over the collection, propagation and distribution of various seed types throughout the states.

But in 1883, professionals in the seed industry formed the American Seed Trade Association and began lobbying for private seed development. The endeavor finally succeeded in 1924, and soon the industry would see new avenues opening with the development of hybrids and the strong spurt in seed trade following World War II. Americans could grow their own fruits and vegetables with increasingly relative ease, and eventually the country that once desperately sought seeds was home to the world's largest commercial seed industry—talk about a growing market.

4

FIG

"And Judah and Israel dwelt safely, every man under his vine and under his fig tree, from Dan even to Beersheba, all the days of Solomon."
— *The King James Bible (1 Kings 4:25)*

IN BIBLICAL TIMES, figs represented prosperity. Today, the ancient fruit is likely to be described as "divine," as they're frequently found either chocolate-dipped, prosciutto-wrapped or in their more populist "Newton" form.

The fig originated in Asia Minor and began spreading through the Mediterranean region thanks to the likes of the Greeks and the Romans. In the 1500s, Spanish Franciscan missionaries brought the fruit to what is now southern California. The Golden State currently produces the majority of the country's figs, making varieties such as Black Mission, Calimyrna and Kadota abundant. Still, figgy pudding continues to elude Christmas carolers everywhere.

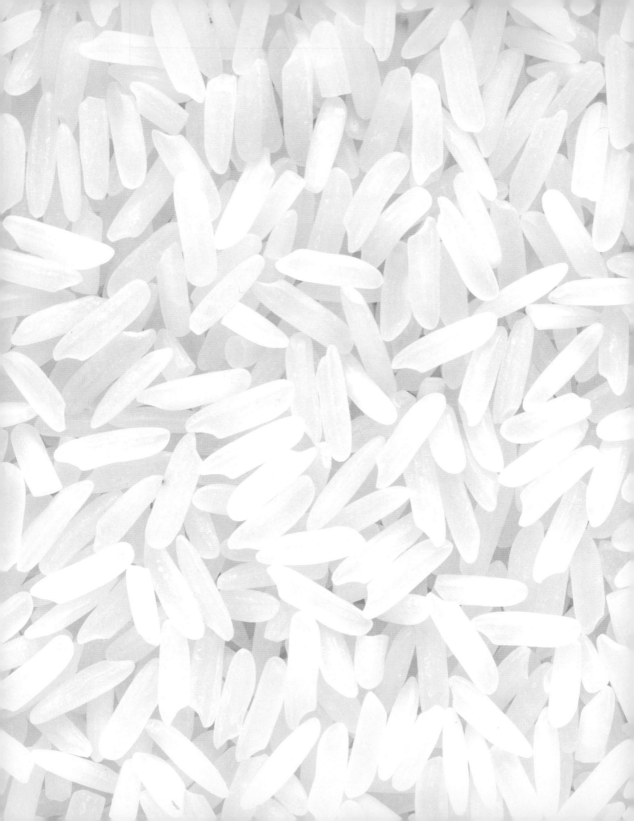

RICE

NO CROP IN human history has been a more versatile, widespread source of sustenance than rice. The initial domestication of the grain's two main subspecies, indica and japonica, can be traced back roughly 8,200 to 13,500 years ago to the Pearl River Valley region in China. For several centuries, rice crops spread throughout Asia and into Europe and Africa. Between the 15th and 17th centuries, during Europe's Age of Exploration, rice was brought to the New World. In the mid-18th century, slaves from West Africa brought the complex farming methods and technologies necessary for mass rice production to the Carolinas, and a fast-rising industry soon followed. By the 20th century, rice was being produced in California's Sacramento Valley right around the same time the first successful crop arrived in Australia.

The starchy dish is now a staple in cuisine from nearly every continent. Rice milk, rice cakes and rice statues have proven the grain's malleability, and it's also perfect for throwing at newlyweds at the end of a wedding. Some believe rice can even save a soaked cell phone from water-logged failure, though these claims have been largely debunked.

6

SILOS

"Much like a lighthouse marks the shoreline, each silo boldly marked where a farmer lived his life and earned his living. Silos were often the first, and sometimes only, indication that someone was farming beyond the next rise on the prairie."
—The Farmers' Tower: The Development of the Tower Silo *by Loran Berg*

THESE ICONIC AGRICULTURAL landmarks first came about in the late 19th century as a means of storing silage, a fodder for cows and sheep that must be fermented and kept moist. For easier unloading, many early silos were deep pits, essentially inverted versions of the tower types. Until the 1890s, most silos were wooden, rectangular structures. But because silage would often get caught in the corners, silos were redesigned to the cylindrical versions seen today. In New England in the late 1800s, farmers began using silos to store corn—regardless of maturity—because it was a higher quality feed for cows and could yield more crops per acre. The years that followed would see a boom in the agricultural industry, with much thanks owed to the rise of silos.

SAKIA

AS EARLY AS 500 B.C., the sakia, also known as the Persian water wheel, provided a means of obtaining water in areas distant from lakes and rivers. Running over two pulley systems, the mechanism consisted of numerous pots and buckets on a long rope. The sakia was powered by animals, typically oxen, who pulled the rope to move a cogged wheel that dipped the pots and buckets into the water supply to be filled.

Declining groundwater levels became an existential threat to the sakia over time. One such Persian water wheel in Kolar, Karnataka, India, at nearly a century old, was temporarily out of commission in 2007 when the area's water table fell too low for the wheel to reach. The mechanism's subsequent preservation is owed to an organization known as the Rainwater Club, which works with farmers to provide efficient means of obtaining and using water. While the archaic sakia lacked the efficiency and reliability of modern variants, it laid the groundwork for future means of irrigation.

PLOW

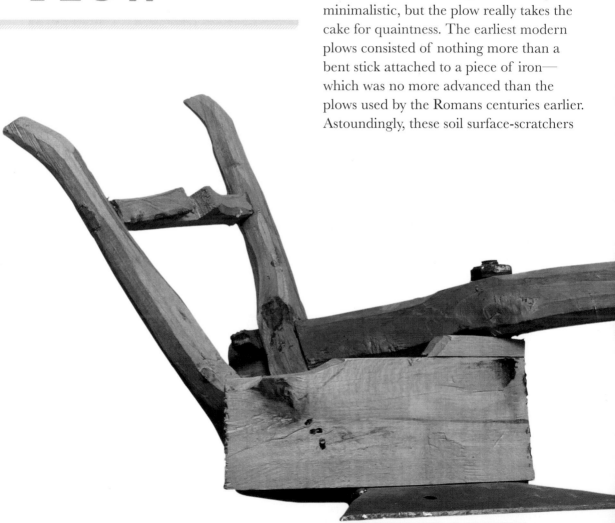

IT'S SAFE TO ASSUME that the earliest forms of farming tools were quite minimalistic, but the plow really takes the cake for quaintness. The earliest modern plows consisted of nothing more than a bent stick attached to a piece of iron—which was no more advanced than the plows used by the Romans centuries earlier. Astoundingly, these soil surface-scratchers would remain in use as late as 1812 until a blacksmith named Jethro Wood created a cast iron plow consisting of three separate parts. This allowed for broken parts to be easily replaced in lieu of buying an entirely new plow. The next major advancement came from one of the most famous names in farming equipment today, John Deere, whose 1837 "grasshopper plows" allowed farmers to easily cut through hardened prairie ground.

In the 1840s, the arrival of the sulky plow allowed farmers to sit and ride rather than walk alongside the plow. Animals were gradually given a break, too, as farm tractors later became the plow pullers, allowing American agriculture to become far more efficient and meet the country's demand for homegrown foods.

MASON JAR

WHILE MASON JARS may be the go-to candle holder or beverage vessel for millennials, they were not always a twee accessory. In 1858, John Landis Mason of New Jersey designed a glass to improve the canning process of the time. With a ribbed neck and a cap that screwed on to ensure an airtight seal, Mason's design displayed obvious advantages to previous canning containers. Plus, the transparent glasses offered the perk of the stored food being fully visible. The appeal of Mason jars caught on quickly, and by the 20th century, the Ball Corporation became the most prominent manufacturer and yielded the container's ubiquity.

When World War II broke out, Americans were encouraged to grow their own food while the government implemented a rationing strategy. This led to a surge in the sales of Mason jars as people practiced preservation with one of the most tried and trusted tools for the process. In the '60s and '70s, Mason jars experienced another renaissance as many health-conscious individuals rebelled against the rise of processed foods in favor

of homegrown goods. Mason jars are seeing similar popularity amid the rise of farmers markets and the growing preference for local, organic foods. And who doesn't like getting a jar of homemade jam as a gift?

STEAM-POWERED FARM EQUIPMENT

"It is my prediction that every part of agriculture might be performed by steam."
—Inventor Richard Trevithick, 1812

WHETHER HE WAS psychic or simply had a knack for seeing the potential in technology, Trevithick was right. In 1818, on large sugarcane plantations in Louisiana, steam-powered, stationary engines began driving the mills used to grind cane. Soon after, plantation owners began finding other uses for the costly investment, powering their sawmills and fanning mills with the new technology. Around 1830, rice production was boosted after select rice threshing machines began implementing steam power. As steam power's place in the farming industry continued to reveal itself, the need for steam engines designed specifically for agricultural use became apparent. Recognizing that need, Philadelphia resident A. L. Archambault built what is considered the first portable farm steam engine, called "The Forty-Niner" in 1849. Farmers who had not

yet been onboard began seeing what they were missing out on, and by the early 1900s, dozens of companies were producing thousands of steam-powered engines. With a major increase in productivity, it was full-steam ahead for the agricultural industry.

11

CROP DUSTER

GENERALLY, people dislike bugs interfering with their food (stay out of this, chocolate-covered crickets). And farmers particularly dislike bugs interfering with food, especially because they often keep it from reaching its full potential. But thanks to an experiment conducted by the Ohio Department of Agriculture in 1921, the protection of growing crops from pesky insects is now a manageable task.

Flying a Curtiss JN-6 "Super Jenny" plane under the instructions of the Ohio Department of Agriculture, a U.S. Army pilot named John A. Macready spread lead arsenate dust—which was used to kill sphinx moth larvae—over catalpa trees. The experiment's success led to the first commercial crop dusting in 1923, which was administered by a modified aircraft created by Huff-Daland Dusters, which later became Delta Airlines. From there, crop dusting became an agricultural routine.

The term "dusting" came about due to the types of pesticides used in the early days of the process. Most insecticides were dry, and thus caused a dust-like effect when aerially spread over fields. The U.S. agriculture industry today continues to rely on what has become known as aerial application as it allows for the delivery of up to one-fourth of all crop products.

Essential Appliances

Once various innovations allowed food production to become more efficient, humans sought ways to improve the process of preparing meals at home. And once these items became readily available, they were difficult to live without.

WOOD-FIRED OVEN

OFTEN THE PREFERRED heating source for specialty pizza today, the wood-fired oven was invented at least 7,000 years ago in Ancient Greece. Initially only one kind of leavened loaf was baked, but by the fifth century, they were being used to make hundreds of different kinds of bread, from whole wheat loaves to pizza pies.

Today, the wood-fired oven is practically a modern miracle. No other appliance or culinary tool can bring the heat the way this oven does—at its hottest, a wood-fired oven can reach 1,000 degrees! And the flavor and crispiness it brings to the crust of one of America's most frequently eaten dishes? That's amore.

13

GAS STOVE

DURING THE HEIGHT of the Industrial Revolution in Great Britain, James Sharp filed a patent for the gas stove in 1826. Before this, the English were reliant on wood-fired stoves to warm their meals. Sharp's stove would be marketed by the Smith & Phillips firm beginning in 1828, catalyzing a small culinary revolution. The new stoves allowed meals to be cooked more evenly, and also alleviated the need to constantly stoke or relight a wood-fired stove. Multi-faceted artist

William Hadaway would then turn up the heat in 1896 with his patent for the electric stove, which was made possible by Thomas Ahearn's electric range model. The years that followed saw a strong marketing push for electric stoves, despite some traditionalists arguing that the new contraptions took away from the art of cooking. By the 1920s, electric stoves began edging wood-fired stoves out of the marketplace, eventually replacing them in many homes.

KELVINATOR REFRIGERATOR

TODAY, REFRIGERATORS ARE chilling in supermarkets, offices, kitchens, dorm rooms, garages and anywhere else chilled food is needed. But for people living in the early 1900s, this ease of access to chilled food and ice cubes would have been an unimaginable luxury. Before 1918, only the meatpacking, dairy and fishing industries had access to electric refrigeration. Some homes were lucky enough to have ice boxes, and even they would have to buy pounds of ice daily from an "ice man."

But in 1925, the purveyors of ice could hang up their caps because the first electric refrigerator, named the Kelvinator, hit the market. From then on, homeowners had an easy means of storing their perishable foods. The innovation, of course, also gave way to the classic line, "Is your refrigerator running?"—a joke that has caused eyes to roll for nearly a century now.

WATERS-GENTER COMPANY'S MODEL 1-A-1 TOASTMASTER

WHAT WOULD BREAKFAST BE WITHOUT TOAST? This sliced, browned piece of bread has been a mainstay throughout human history. Originally held over the fire like a marshmallow or cooked in an oven, the way people made toast stayed relatively the same for thousands of years—until the toastmaster came along and changed the norm.

In 1920, a Minnesota man named Charles Strite was sick of seeing burnt toast in his cafeteria every day, so he decided to do something about it. A year later, he filed a patent for the first electric, pop-up toaster. Strite formed the Waters-Genter Company to create the first Toastmaster in 1926, revolutionizing breakfast everywhere and giving the world the best thing to happen to bread since pre-sliced loaves.

RADARANGE MICROWAVE

WHETHER HEATING UP a frozen dinner or reviving a meal from the night before, microwaves have been saving people from putting in the full effort of cooking meals for decades. Now a preferred part of everyday life, this invention was actually unintentionally stumbled upon by scientists during World War II.

When Raytheon engineer Percy Spencer watched a radar demonstration, he felt a peanut bar in his pocket start cooking and his curiosity was piqued. Eager for another test, Spencer put an uncooked egg into a kettle and placed it near the contained radar rays. As he looked in to see if the egg was frying, it exploded in his face. It was truly an "Aha!" moment, but the technology took years to perfect.

By 1946, Spencer had filed a patent demonstrating that this technology could cause the kernels of popcorn to pop right off the cob. Although this new way to cook was truly miraculous, the first version of the microwave, called the Radarange (pictured), was not meant for American homes. Standing more than 5 feet tall and costing more than $1,200, the Radarange was initially only marketed to restaurants and airlines. It would be another 25 years until the consumer microwave fully revolutionized the American kitchen.

Basic Culinary Items

From culture to culture and kitchen to kitchen, certain objects have become necessary to meet the standards—and preserve the history—of various cuisines.

CURRY POT

SPICINESS, WHILE sometimes polarizing among food lovers, is a signature trait of countless cuisines across the globe. Its many incarnations often overlap, creating a common thread between otherwise disparate dishes. Curry, a favorite among those with a hunger for heat and great flavor, is so essential to some regional cooking that it even has its own pot.

Sri Lanka has been cooking with curry for centuries due to its long history as a trading post and producer of spice. In the island nation, curry and sauce are basically one and the same, which means most spicy dishes are given the label of "curry." Throughout its history, Sri Lankans have cooked their curry dishes in rounded clay pots known as "walang." Chunks of chicken, fish and garlic in spicy sauces are commonly made in these pots as they are placed directly on flames. With the convenience of making an entire meal at once in just one dish, the walang is almost something like an ancient slow cooker. Today, the ancient curry pot is still used by Sri Lankan traditionalists looking to fire up authentic cuisine.

MORTAR AND PESTLE

WHILE MANY OF history's earliest culinary items have undergone a complete aesthetic overhaul since their creation, the mortar and pestle still looks like its old self. This tandem of tools has been put to a wide variety of uses between the time of its inception thousands of years ago to present day.

The mortar and pestle you might use to turn basil and pine nuts into pesto in a cooking class likely looks very similar to the 6,000-year-old tool discovered in Mexico's Tehuacan Valley or similar objects used by the ancient Greeks, the Aztecs, the Egyptians and the Romans. And because the mortar and pestle was discovered to be useful in preparing medicinal oils and tinctures, it can even be seen in logos for Walgreens drugstores.

Whether being used to grind up spices or whip up guacamole, the mortar and pestle's virtually unchanged design is a testament to its efficacy. When it comes to the craft of cooking, sometimes a little elbow grease goes a long way.

19

WOK

THE IMAGE OF a flame-engulfed wok filled with meats and veggies is one any Chinese restaurant-goer knows well. And this effective, spacious cookware is no novel innovation, but rather one that has been serving the culinary world well for centuries.

While its exact date of origin has been debated by historians, the wok—which translates to "cooking pot" in Cantonese—became prominent roughly 2,000 years ago in China. The inspiration for the wok likely came from India, where similar pans known as kuali were used frequently to cook food over an open fire. Early Chinese woks were made by repeatedly heating and cooling ceramic molds over a period of several days, but the process would eventually be improved with the availability of high-silicon foundry iron in the 19th century. The innovation led to woks that were far faster to produce and more durable, allowing cooks to stir fry, sauté and deep fry countless dishes in a single night. And as Chinese cuisine became a staple of American eating, the wok ensured take-out chefs an efficient means of making multiple meals at once.

ANCIENT CAULDRON

IT MAY BE more closely associated with witches, warlocks and *Harry Potter* these days, but the cauldron was once as commonplace in cooking as a boiling pot. In fact, that's essentially what they were just much larger and far less convenient.

In the Middle Ages, cauldrons were nearly essential as their versatility allowed for the cooking of everything from soups to casseroles over an open flame. Most were made of cast iron, but come the 17th century, cauldrons made of brass became a hot item. In the county town of Taunton in Somerset,

England, brass cauldrons were typically owned by rich merchants who often obtained them via long-distance trades. One foundry in the Taunton area, known as Fathers Foundry, capitalized on the demand for the domestic cookware and began producing cauldrons, skillets and mortars marked with an "IF" insigna, and one such cauldron from 1692 can be found in the Marazion Museum in Cornwall, England, today. Between their built-in desirability and the rise of brand names, brass cauldrons were essentially an early equivalent of a Williams Sonoma boiling pot.

21

CAST-IRON FRYING PAN

ONE OF THE MOST useful tools in any kitchen, the cast-iron frying pan can cook just about anything. And though it might seem like a modern miracle, the cast-iron pan was invented nearly 2,000 years ago.

The ancient Chinese used these seemingly invincible frying pans to cook, as did the Romans. In a 14th-century cookbook called Apicuis's *De re Coquinaria*, the frying pan was even dubbed an essential item. And despite centuries passing, the cast-iron pan has remained relatively unchanged. Boasting both durability and versatility, the cookware is commonly passed down within American families, and some modern home cooks are likely to be sizzling a steak in the same pan their grandfather used to cook cornbread. Those who don't receive such an heirloom for their stovetop are likely to slot a cast-iron pan at the top of their wedding gift wish list, perhaps in an effort to start a family tradition of their own.

22

SILVER TEAPOT

WHILE SIPPING TEA from a ceramic teacup might seem like something reserved for the Queen of England, the practice was not actually conceived in Europe. The teapot was invented in China during the Yuan dynasty, some time between the years of 1271 and 1368. Usually made of bronze or silver, the teapot was first described in a text from that time, titled *Jiyuan Conghua*.

But it wouldn't be until the late 1600s that tea would arrive on European soil. Then considered a luxury item, the most stylish way to display tea was in porcelain teapots. They were exclusively made in China and could withstand corrosive salt water, which was important because teapots were transported by sea. But as trends changed, everyone was all about silver, and there was an ideal place from which to get it—a city in the American colonies that would later be associated with tea for different reasons.

Boston was renowned for its production of silver and by the mid-1700s, silver teapots were being sent over to Europe by the ship-load. And though tea is no longer considered a luxury, drinking tea from a teapot set still holds a certain elegance for everyone, from little girls in playhouses to grown adults in posh neighborhood cafes.

SUSHI MAT

SUSHI FIRST AROSE in 8th-century Japan as a method for preserving fish in fermented rice. Only the raw fish would be eaten, because the rice served only as a protective covering. The Edo Period during the 18th century sparked a new movement in which the rice and fish were assembled with vinegar and vegetables to be eaten all at once. With the invention of nori seaweed in sheet form, it proved to be the perfect component in bringing all the ingredients together. Chefs would skillfully pack and roll everything together using bamboo mats, forming the modern sushi rolls enjoyed today. Because the sushi mat allowed for the food to be compressed into bite-sized pieces, sushi quickly became an early form of fast food, with street vendors selling it outdoors to be eaten on the go.

In the early 1970s, sushi started to become popular in the United States. Cities such as L.A. and New York were host to the first American sushi restaurants. Today, the Japanese fast food can be found almost anywhere, and it can also be made at home with a few simple ingredients and a bamboo rolling mat.

CHRISTMAS COOKIE CUTTER

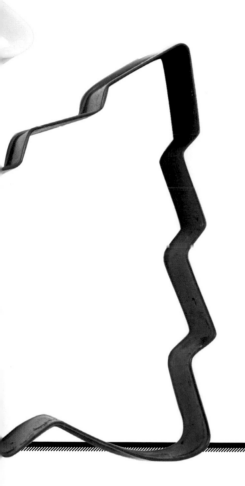

THE USE OF cookie cutters dates as far back as 2000 B.C., when Ancient Egyptians used a variety of wooden and ceramic molds for baking. It wasn't until the 16th century, however, that these decorative molds or cutters became essential to the Christmas season. The most iconic of Christmas cookie shapes is the gingerbread man—a staple that was invented by Queen Elizabeth I. Gingerbread was already popular, but Elizabeth I had her cookies designed and shaped in the likeness of her dignified guests. Bakers around Europe would be swamped with requests for these new treats, and they began using tin cookie cutters to speed up the process. In the 16th century, decorated gingerbread houses were already a Christmas tradition in Germany, and so their gingerbread men counterparts quickly became associated with the holiday season as well. Europeans would later bring their Christmas traditions to the United States, where the cookie cutters eventually expanded to include a variety of seasonal shapes.

BUTCHER KNIFE

WITH CUTTING CAPABILITIES that are constantly being improved upon, the butcher knife is an indispensable tool of modern meat preparation. These wide-blade knives were used by trappers and explorers living in the North American territory. Most of these "mountain men" were employed by major fur trading companies and used the knives for skinning and cutting meat. By the early 1800s, cutlery crafters began selling the tools as "butcher" knives, giving butchers—who had previously been using smaller, weaker knives—an efficient and rugged-looking means of breaking down meat products.

Now found in kitchens and restaurants rather than the American frontier, the heftier curved blade is still used to strip and cut meat. There have also been many descendents of the butcher knife since its inception—with the chef's knife, carving knife and cleaver also used in the butchering process. And though meat preparation has historically been done by hand by trained butchers in butcher shops, these speciality shops have decreased in popularity due to the rise of supermarkets. It's now more common for supermarket meat to be "case-ready," in which the product is prepared and packaged in an industrial plant—making way for mass produced processed meats, and leaving the butcher knife in the hands of chefs.

CAN OPENER

WITHOUT THIS VITAL TOOL, forget about opening your soup, vegetables or canned bread (if you're inclined to eat such a thing). Canned food was first conceived by French chef Nicolas Appert in 1810, after Napoleon offered a reward to anyone who could figure out a way to preserve food to feed his hungry soldiers. But it would be decades before an official opening device was invented. In the meantime, soldiers had to puncture the tin can lid with their bayonets in order to access the meats and vegetables preserved inside. Unfortunately for Appert, his groundbreaking invention was too far ahead of its time. People weren't interested in canned foods, and the inventor died nearly penniless, passing away before canning took off.

Finally, in 1858, Connecticut native Ezra Warner filed a patent for the can opener, making preserved goods far more convenient.

Almost 20 years after Appert's death, the American Civil War broke out in 1861, and canning was necessary to feed both sides. Canned goods—and subsequently, can openers—became a permanent fixture in U.S. pantries. A 2013 survey conducted by the Cans Get You Cooking program revealed 98 percent of American kitchens are stocked with canned goods at all times.

27

TURKEY BASTER

EVERY FOURTH Thursday of November, Americans gather with family and friends to consume a massive feast commemorating the breaking of bread between pilgrims and Native Americans. But anyone responsible for preparing the Thanksgiving meal knows this heavenly celebration of peace can be hell to put together. Since Abraham Lincoln declared Thanksgiving a national holiday on October 3, 1863, hapless chefs have battled the terror of dry turkey for generations. While our 19th-century predecessors had to rely on unwieldy and clumsy ladles to baste the bird—covering it in its own juices to give the skin a crisp, golden coating— the industrialization and popularization of vulcanized rubber gave rise to today's turkey baster. Using the simple principle of suction, this tool helps make preparing for the big day just a little easier, allowing cooks to easily transfer juices from the pan to the turkey and focus on more important things—like keeping Uncle Earl from having that fifth glass of wine.

28

GLASS MILK BOTTLE

THE IMAGE OF A milkman delivering a cold glass bottle to a suburban house inspires nostalgia for early 20th-century America. As delightfully quaint as it seems, milk delivery was necessary in the days before refrigerators had become a standard appliance. As a result, milk would truly go from farm to table.

Before glass milk bottles, milkmen would have to pour milk into customers' jugs from trucks and come around several times a day. But that changed in 1878, when George Lester patented the first glass milk bottle in New York. That invention, paired with pasteurization in 1864, meant milkmen only needed to come around once a day with their farm-filled bottles, and it remained that way for decades.

With the advent of refrigerators in the '50s and the rise of supermarkets, the milkman became scarce. Milk bottles have since become collectibles for antique enthusiasts, but in some communities the farm-to-table movement is putting milkmen back to work, all for the sake of fresher dairy.

Innovations

Throughout history, humans have never ceased their quest to make food easier to obtain and prepare. This resulted in many outside-the-box creations and, in some cases, better tasting food.

29

FISH HOOK

IN 2005, *Forbes* named the fish hook one of the top 20 tools in history because it can provide a simple, effective means of gathering food and income that became so indispensable it evolved civilization. The earliest known hook used to bring fish from sea to land was discovered at the southern end of Okinawa Island. Archaeologists discovered the hook was made from sea snail shell and was 23,000 years old. Another early fish hook, made from a whittled down bone with a groove in the middle for a string to be tied, was unearthed in France and believed to be about 7,000 years old. These hooks were often straight; hooks didn't gain their modern bent shape until around 3000 B.C. in the First Egyptian Dynasty.

When angling emerged as a popular sport in 15th-century England, crudely bent needles began to be manufactured and marketed as fish hooks. One of the first companies to make quality, mass-produced fishing hooks in the shape we know today was the Mustad Company, founded in Gjörvik, Norway, in 1832. Tackle has grown more varied, yet the classic hooked design remains intact, casting a line between modern anglers and their early human ancestors.

30

SUGARCANE PLANT

AS THE BEARER of one of the most irresistible ingredients known to man, it's no surprise the sugarcane plant was something the whole world wanted to get its hands on. First cultivated in New Guinea around 6000 B.C., sugarcane gradually made its way westward with Arabian traders in the 7th century. Once attached to Western civilization, sugar production spread throughout the Mediterranean and North Africa, until it landed in Europe as a result of the crusade in the 11th century. Crusaders had never tasted anything quite like it and considered cane sugar a "new spice."

The 15th century brought sugar to the New World when Christopher Columbus first carried sugarcane to the Caribbean during his second trip to America. When Caribbean slave farmers crushed the sugarcane and boiled its juices in clay pots, a liquid now known as molasses—would leak out. Eventually, it was discovered that molasses could be combined with the fermented cane liquid to create an alcohol, which came to be known as rum. By the 16th century, slave labor was utilized on most cane fields, leading to the arrival of millions of Africans to the Americas. Sugar trade profits soared, and even long after America gained independence from Great Britain and slavery was later abolished, the crop continued to be extremely valuable, making its way into soda, confections, coffee and just about everything else.

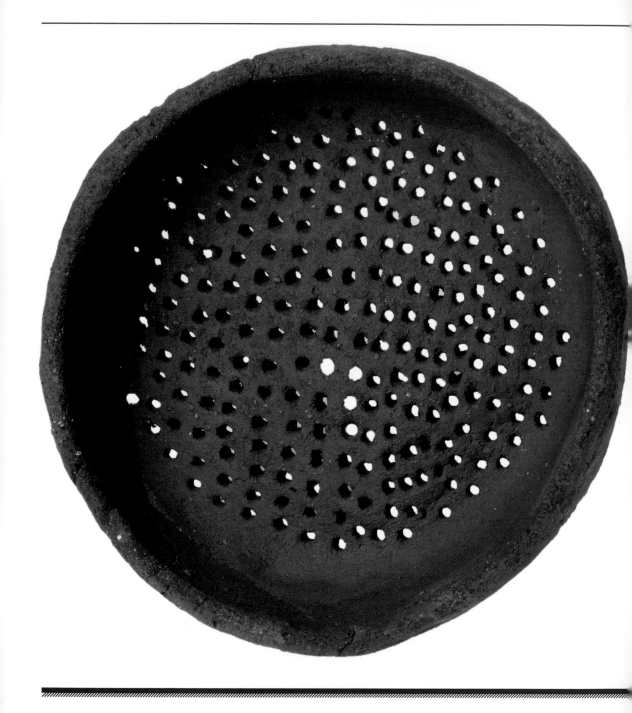

31

CHEESE STRAINER

"The presence of milk residues in sieves—which look like modern cheese-strainers—constitutes the earliest direct evidence for cheese-making."
—Mélanie Roffet-Salque

IN 2012, ROFFET-SALQUE and several other University of Bristol researchers and professors reported evidence suggesting the earliest instances of cheese-making date back roughly 7,500 years ago to the region of Kuyavia in Poland. The evidence consisted of several hole-laden pieces of pottery containing high levels of milk-fat residue, suggesting they were sieves used as cheese strainers. After the discovery in Poland, Princeton University archaeologist Peter Bogucki noted that the 19th-century perforated ceramics he observed in Vermont—which were also used for cheese-making—strongly resembled those from 7,500 years ago.

Cheese as we know it today is among the most versatile foods at our disposal. Whether it's a slice of Swiss melted over a burger, a platter of Brie served at a cocktail party or some mascarpone served with a little honey and almond as dessert, there's a cheese for every occasion—all thanks to a process that's been perfected over thousands of years.

FORK

WHILE IT MAY seem like one of the most rudimentary tools we have at our daily disposal, the fork has only been bringing food to faces for hundreds of years, rather than thousands. Two-pronged utensils were used within the Byzantine Empire as early as the 11th century, but since the fork resembled—and got its name from—the devil's pitchfork, it remained a tough sell for centuries.

32

After making its way into Italy, the fork would get a chance to shine thanks to Catherine de Medici in 1533. Following her arrival in France to marry Henry II, Catherine toured all around displaying her dining etiquette at festivals where she would use a fork for many different dishes. The utensil would retain its upper class status would for much of the 17th and 18th centuries until cutlery sets began appearing in homes regularly, now with three and four-pronged forks. With the arrival of silver-plating technology, mass-production of affordable forks became possible, and they soon could be purchased for all households.

33

OIL PRESS

WHETHER IT'S COATING a frying pan, serving as a salad dressing or being used as a dip for fresh-baked bread, olive oil is one of the most fundamental culinary components today. Long before city dwellers were traveling to the local Greek grocery store to buy bottles of the best brands, oil press machines were making the popular product possible.

The process of crushing olives into oil began around 2500 B.C., with the fatty liquid serving a variety of uses, from lamp fuel to medicinal ointment. The original method involved placing the olives in either a woven basket or sack, crushing the contents, pouring hot water over the basket or sack and then placing all of the resulting oily liquid in a reservoir to settle and separate before being skimmed and stored. The Romans and Greeks would later improve the process by creating several incarnations of oil press machines, which featured levels and counterweights that crushed the baskets and sacks far more efficiently. Around 200 B.C., the Romans spearheaded the industrialization of olive oil, and production of the product caught on quickly from there. In the centuries that followed, production of olive oil would increase by millions—and eventually, billions—of liters per year.

34

COFFEE GRINDER

SURE, GRINDING ONE'S own beans may be seen as extraneous labor to many modern coffee drinkers, but that work was unavoidable in the pre-café world. Those in Turkey and Persia in the 1400s would adapt a hand-cranked spice grinder for coffee bean grinding purposes, the first to introduce the mechanism to the process. By 1778, coffee processing innovations were so integral to the Spanish economy that Charles III banned all exports of hand-cranked coffee grinders to the United States.

The U.S. was ultimately unphased by being cut off from new developments in coffee grinding from Europe, and the first U.S. coffee grinder patent would be issued in 1798 to Maryland resident Thomas Bruff, who also happened to be Thomas Jefferson's dentist. Perhaps inspired by his patients grinding their teeth, Bruff's device was wall-mounted and used metal nuts with textured teeth to grind the beans. The following century would see the arrival of packaged, ground coffee in 1860, followed by John Gulick Baker's Champion #1 grinder a decade later, which became the go-to model for grocery stores across the country.

35

SHIP

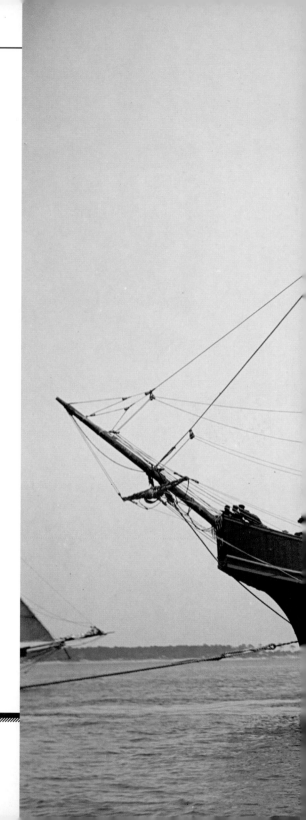

WITHOUT THIS timeless mode of transportation, so many of the world's most beloved crops, spices and sundry goods would have remained isolated in their places of origin rather than becoming exports. And because life on a ship created countless challenges for early voyagers—particularly concerning the safety of stored foods—the value of preserved goods became increasingly clear.

Between the years of 1500 and 1800, more than 2 million sailors died from scurvy, which is caused by a severe lack of vitamin C. But in the 1760s, Captain James Cook's crew discovered that fermented cabbage, typically known as sauerkraut, was a reliable defense against the illness since it contained plenty of vitamin C and could be kept at room temperature for months at a time. In the case of the ship, limitations actually yielded a culinary innovation.

SPICE JAR

NO MATTER what you're eating, there's a good chance you enhanced its flavor with the likes of salt, pepper, paprika or something else on your spice rack. Spices have been used to flavor foods since the early days of global civilization, with the spice trade connecting continents through the shared desire for these goods. For many years, though, the spice trade was largely ineffective due to transactions taking place via camel caravan. In other words, if you were in Asia hoping to get spices from North Africa, it was going to be a while. Because of how difficult they were to obtain, spices—even pepper—were as valuable as glittering jewels.

In 1498, King João II sent Portuguese explorer Vasco da Gama to discover a more efficient sea-based trade route around India and Africa and to bring back as many spices as he could. While some romantics might focus on the breathtaking opportunity navigating uncharted waters presents, the proposition could have easily become a lifetaking one. By some miracle, not only did da Gama survive the dangerous endeavor, he also brought back boatloads of spices from India's Malabar Coast, and was sent back in 1502 to barter for more. While people don't typically risk their lives for spices today, they're still an essential for food lovers.

FEEDING TUBE

IN THE EVENT of an illness or a temporary side effect of surgery, feeding tubes are used to supply nutrients to those who are unable to eat. Known as enteral nutrition, a variety of different tubes and placements are used in the process to deliver liquid food formulas. Modern tubes are usually placed through the nose (nasogastric tubes) or directly through the skin (gastrostomy) into the small bowel or stomach. Now a common tool in medical practice, this alternative method of consuming nutrients has been in the making for thousands of years.

The earliest type of enteral feeding dates all the way back to a 3,500-year-old piece of papyrus that revealed Ancient Egyptians and Greeks used enemas infused with nutrients to preserve their health. These early solutions were made from wine, milk, wheat, eggs and, later, brandy. The upper GI tract was difficult to access and wasn't used for feeding until 1598 when Venetian doctor Capivacceus used a hollow tube to push liquids down the esophagus. From there, doctors spent centuries experimenting with and finessing tube size, weight, entry points and proteins in the formulas in order to make enteral feeding a reality for those in need of a healthy alternative.

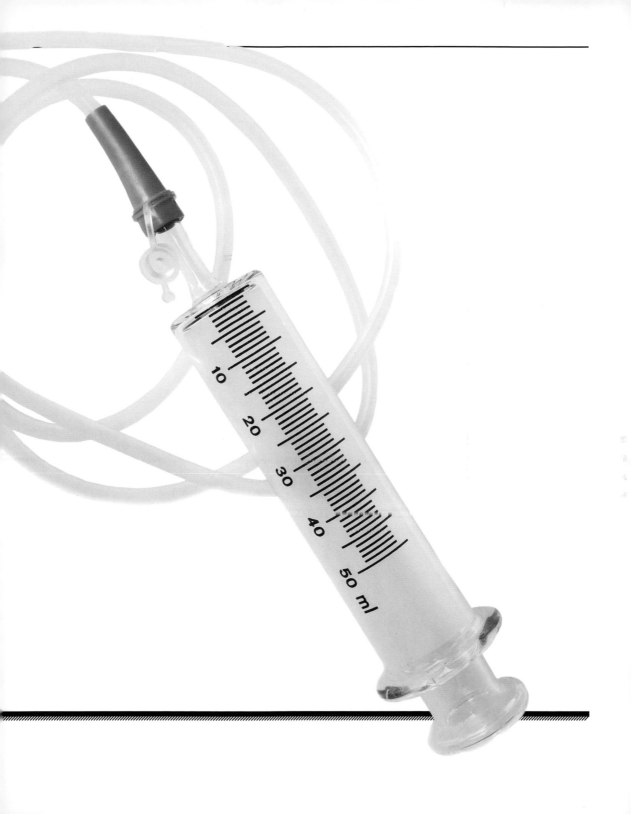

PASTA MAKER

THE 1600S ARE considered the Golden Age of pasta manufacturing, with the invention of the extrusion press yielding many new production plants along the coast of San Remo, Italy. Along with the obvious benefit of efficiency, the consistency from piece to piece was considered one of the greatest advantages of machine-made pasta. Extrusion presses would quickly make their way across the country with manufacturers seeing great success from the machine. In 1848, Brooklyn, New York, would become home to the first pasta manufacturing plant in America, Zerega's Sons, Inc. Founder Antoine Zerega's descendants continue to operate the business, now headquartered in New Jersey. A device with proven longevity, pasta makers allow everyone from restaurant chefs to home cooks to create one of history's most beloved dishes with ease, and gift registries for weddings of all stripes often include one—even if it's just to say you own something that's been in its box since your nuptials.

SANDWICH

"Enjoy every sandwich."

—Warren Zevon

THIS STATEMENT, spoken by a legendary musician on *The Late Show with Dave Letterman* in his dying days, serves as a lesson in appreciating life's simple pleasures—which, for many, are food-related. The sandwich, in its seemingly infinite forms, is one of the most universally appreciated forms of culinary convenience, and its history is as stacked as a turkey club.

While the genius combination of bread, meat and various fillings has been experimented with since ancient times, the true birth of the sandwich is supposed to have occurred in England in 1762. During a lengthy gambling binge, John Montagu, 4th Earl of Sandwich, asked his cook for something he could eat utensil-free to avoid interference with his game. The cook returned with meat wedged between two pieces of toasted bread, to which Montagu responded enthusiastically. For the remainder of the 18th century, the sandwich was something mostly eaten by England's elite. As for America, it would take until the 1810s before the sandwich gained prominence. But today, it's one of the most ubiquitous foods around, just as welcome in Italian cuisine as Vietnamese cuisine.

40

CUPCAKE PAN

"A muffin is a bald cupcake."

—Jim Gaffigan

THE OFTEN-PREFERRED, frosted cousin of the muffin was first mentioned in Amelia Simmons's 1796 cookbook, *American Cookery*, which included a recipe for "a light cake to bake in small cups." These "cupcakes" eventually became named for what they were baked in—heavy pottery cups or small ceramic bowls. The first cupcake pan originated as a heavy sheet of cast iron with individual cup molds. In 1859, the design was patented by Nathaniel Waterman, who intended the pan be used to bake small gem breads. The pan changed its primary purpose over the years to accommodate the growing popularity of the cupcake as a desert. This began when Hostess became the first to mass-produce CupCakes in 1919. By the 1940s and '50s, simple cake mixes by companies such as Duncan Hines made these store-bought treats both easier and cheaper to make at home. With a growing emphasis on women as homemakers, this brought about a wider variety of cookware products, and Waterman's invention gradually became the metal, nonstick, lightweight pan that's recognizable today.

41

THERMOS

IF YOU'VE EVER ASKED the question, "How does a thermos know whether to keep its contents hot or cold," don't be ashamed—you're far from alone. That inquiry is constantly creeping into curious minds, highlighting the genius of this innovative vessel.

In the mid-1890s, an Oxford University scientist named Sir James Dewar created a "vacuum flask" by placing one bottle inside another, wrapping the inner bottle in foil and pumping out all of the air between the bottles. The container could keep liquids hot—or cold—for hours because the airtight bottles, which absorbed the heat emitted from the contents, encased the liquids in their own heat. In 1904, the "vacuum flask"—now dubbed the thermos after the Greek word "therme," which means "heat"—was commercially manufactured by two German glass blowers, whose firm would become known as Thermos GmbH. But because Dewar never filed a patent, he was denied a profit. And due to "thermos" quickly becoming the generic term for all containers of the sort, Thermos GmbH lost exclusive rights to the name. Despite the circumstances that cooled the heat of its creation, the thermos went on to become one of the most useful vessels today, regularly keeping our coffee, tea and soups at the perfect temperature.

STAND MIXER

EVEN WITH TODAY'S TOOLS, making bread from scratch is no piece of cake. But before the invention of the stand mixer, the process was even more energy-consuming. After observing a baker tediously mixing dough with a metal spoon in 1908, an engineer from Troy, Ohio, named Herbert Johnson quickly created an electric standing mixer to ease the burden of bread making. By 1915, Johnson was selling his 80-quart mixers to more and more professional bakers. The innovation's potential would be further realized just four years later in 1919 when Johnson, now operating under the brand name KitchenAid, introduced a stand mixer to be sold in stores for home bakers. The KitchenAid would only get better from there, receiving a new, sleeker design in 1936 and options for colorful models by 1955. Today, stand mixers—particularly those made by KitchenAid—continue to be an essential tool for professional bakers and a wishlist appliance for aspiring home bakers.

42

43

THE PIGGLY WIGGLY

NO BUILDING better serves as a victory monument to the marvels of modernity than the local supermarket. Row after brightly lit row of shelves packed with an abundance of food, all within an arm's reach, represents the end game in *Homo sapiens*' struggle for sustenance. The supermarket as we know it can be traced to 79 Jefferson Street in Memphis, Tennessee, the home to the first self-service grocery store: The Piggly Wiggly, which opened its doors on September 6, 1916.

Prior to Piggly Wiggly, grocery stores didn't trust Americans to handle their own purchases. Instead, anyone wanting to fill their bare larders and empty cupboard would have to hand a long list to a store clerk, who would then fetch the items and either hand them over to the customer in person or deliver the goods to their home—once they finished the orders put in earlier, of course, a process that could take hours. Piggly Wiggly's method proved a winning strategy, helping the single location grow to a chain of 2,500 stores at its height in the 1930s. While the brand's empire may have shrunk to around 530 stores in operation today, the presentation and method it pioneered has become the shopping experience almost everyone living today has grown up with.

SLICED BREAD

EARLY IN THE 20th century, Missouri-based jeweler Otto Rohwedder invented a machine that would forever raise the bar for all creations to come—at least, as far as the expression "The best thing since sliced bread" is concerned. Rohwedder's initial blueprints and prototype for a bread-slicing machine were destroyed in a fire in 1917, but more than a decade later in 1928, the invention would finally be put to the test at the Chillicothe Baking Company in Chillicothe, Missouri. From there, the popularity of this newfound convenience rose like a loaf in the oven.

By 1930, sliced bread was already the norm across the U.S., with Wonder Bread leading the charge for commercially produced loaves. And nearly a century later, things have hardly changed. When Wonder Bread vanished from grocery store shelves in 2012 due to its then-parent company Hostess Brands filing for bankruptcy, Flower Foods soon came to the brand's rescue, ensuring the continuation of one of the most trusted brands of one of the most beloved food items.

45

DOUGHNUT MACHINE

MANAGING TO PASS as a breakfast food despite having all the attributes of a dessert, the doughnut has been delighting everyone from Homer Simpson to office workers for nearly a century thanks to a largely unsung innovation.

Introduced to the U.S. by Dutch settlers in the early 20th century, doughnuts were initially scarce due to a lack of efficient production. But in 1920, a refugee from Czarist Russia named Adolph Levitt changed the indulgence game for good by creating the first doughnut machine. Levitt's invention was able to produce 80 dozen doughnuts per hour, creating consistent-looking, fried rings of dough via a simple mechanized process. Many bakeries would soon display their new machines so curious customers could watch their treats being made—a practice still in place today at establishments such as Krispy Kreme.

COMBAT RATIONS

NO ONE WOULD EVER expect fine dining on the battlefield, but the meals that fueled soldiers used to be much less balanced than they are today. In the late 19th and early 20th century, military "sustenance" consisted of bare-bones canned goods and dry foods that typically sat in the sun on the back of a wagon for months at a time.

But beginning in World War II, advancements were made in an effort to provide better food for soldiers. The C-ration—containing beef, potatoes, rice or pasta, three biscuits, toffee, instant coffee and sugar cubes—was introduced, along with the emergency D-ration, which contained a candy bar. Combat rations would receive a full overhaul in the 1980s as the tinned food was replaced with airtight bags containing "Meals, Ready to Eat" (MRE). With options for kosher, halal and vegetarian diets, the upgrade accommodated soldiers of varying dietary needs.

47

AEROSOL CAN

THE FIRST USE OF the modern aerosol can—which converts a substance into a fine spray—dates back to World War II, when bug repellent was put into pressurized canisters. These "bug bombs" were used by soldiers to fight mosquitos carrying malaria in the Pacific. When the war ended, a public patent made the can design and chemical propellants available to all kinds of different manufacturers. By the mid-'50s, aerosol cans were used for everything from shaving cream to fake snow. At the same time aerosol cans were rising in popularity, so too was the market for fully prepared and processed foods. These growing trends created the perfect marriage for "push-button" aerosol cuisine. The compressed chemicals were adjusted for human consumption, and short-lived fads in the late '50s yielded numerous foods in sprayable form—cheese, icing, pancake batter and even alcohol.

By the 1970s, Americans were becoming more aware of not only what they were putting in their bodies, but also what they were putting into the environment. A growing hole in the ozone layer was discovered and many of the aerosol can's chemicals became restricted. Remnants of the 1950s aerosol era still remain, however—a quick walk in the grocery store reveals that canned whipped cream and the infamous spreadable cheese have survived over the years.

48

TUPPERWARE

IN 1946, when Earl Silas Tupper introduced his plastic containers with airtight seals, they were not successful. Although the unbreakable containers, spoil-free lids and space saving designs were revolutionary in the market, they didn't sell well in retail stores. It wasn't until Brownie Wise, a single mother from Georgia, discovered selling Tupperware in her home allowed her to earn her own income that the containers began to make their way into kitchen cabinets across the country. Wise began creating a network of women who would sell Tupperware at home parties, a strategy that garnered the attention of creator Earl Tupper himself. Tupper offered Wise the position of VP of Sales in 1951.

At a time when women were conventionally tied to their homes, Wise's Tupperware Parties allowed them to earn their own income on their own time. The popularity of these parties reached new heights when Wise began implementing incentives for sellers. At yearly conventions, top representatives would be awarded prizes such as appliances, boats or vacations. More than 50 years later, women are still holding Tupperware parties around the world. While it was Tupper who invented the containers, it's Brownie Wise who made Tupperware a household name.

49

FONDUE POT

NOTHING QUITE SAYS "life is good" like the decadent act of dipping various foods into melted cheese or chocolate. But before its rise in popularity in recent centuries, such a pleasurable dish was most likely a food lover's dream.

College English majors might recall mentions of a goat cheese, wine and flour mixture in the pages of Homer's epic poem *The Iliad*, but modern fondue—a pot containing melted cheese and wine (or beer)held over an open flame—would not come to any real prominence until the late 1800s in Switzerland. The cheese-producing country would quickly realize the dish's value, though, and in 1930, the Swiss Cheese Union declared fondue the national dish. In 1975, fondue would officially arrive in North America with the founding of The Melting Pot, a chain of fondue restaurants still in operation today throughout the U.S., Canada and Mexico. And with the advent of online retail, anyone can now easily purchase a fondue kit to host a fancy feast of melted cheese or chocolate right in their own home.

DELI SLICER

THE CARVING KNIFE is a useful tool, and it's common knowledge that few things taste better than a thick-carved turkey sandwich the afternoon after Thanksgiving. But before 1898, when Rotterdam pork shop owner Wilhelm Van Berkel invented the first ever food slicer, the simple pleasure of thinly sliced cold cuts on bread was lost upon generations of sandwich eaters beginning with the 4th Earl of Sandwich himself.

Van Berkel's invention, the precursor to every imposing, wheeled slicer in delis, bodegas and luncheonettes all over the world, was the result of a growing demand for pre-sliced meats and cheeses to satisfy the ever-quickening pace of industrial-age life. Today, slicers are found almost anywhere sandwiches are made, which is to say, just about anywhere food is served.

CROCK-POT

FOR HOME COOKS with busy schedules, nothing beats the luxury of leaving food to cook itself throughout the day or overnight. In 1940, inventor Irving Naxon received the patent for his portable cooking device featuring both a cooking vessel and a heating element. Naxon credited the inspiration to his grandmother who, while working at a bakery in Lithuania, made a dish that she cooked overnight in the lingering heat of the bread oven. Known as the Naxon Beanery, the slow cooker arrived on the market in the 1950s, bringing a new wave of convenience to home kitchens. Rival Manufacturing would later acquire Naxon and in 1971, the Beanery was rebranded as the Crock-Pot. For just $25—a slow cooker price that can actually be beaten today—buyers would receive not just a Crock-Pot, but also a complementary Crock-Pot cookbook. Today, hundreds of cookbooks, publications and websites exist for the sole purpose of helping home cooks make everything from oatmeal to Chicken Florentine simply by tossing a few ingredients in their slow cooker.

52

PLASTICWARE

IN 1908, A PUBLIC health officer in Kansas named Dr. Samuel Crumbine spotted one of his tuberculosis patients drinking from a shared cup and water bucket on a train. When the patient was finished, a young girl proceeded to drink from the same cup. This began Crumbine's crusade to ban publically shared drinking and eating utensils (his other campaign was controlling fly-borne diseases and he is also credited with the invention of the fly-swatter). Later that year, an article published by Alvin Davison in *Technical World Magazine* titled "Death in School Drinking Cups" confirmed everything Crumbine was concerned about.

As the spreading of germs became a public concern, Lawrence Luellen and Hugh Moore created the single-use Dixie Cup (called the Health Kup until 1919), which eventually led to a variety of paper and wooden disposable kitchen ware. After World War II, plastic became the preferred material as it was more durable, could be designed in a variety of shapes, and was also able to better maintain the temperature of the food or beverage. Polystyrene is currently the most common type of plastic used in disposable foodservice products including cutlery, cups, plates, containers and trays.

53

DEEP FRYER

"Some people are chocolate and sweets people. I love french fries."
—*Cameron Diaz*

WHILE IT MAY not be just what the doctor ordered, fried food is a staple of most American diets. Frying foods in oil has been a culinary practice for as long as frying pans have been available, with the likes of french fries gradually emerging from experimental batches of fried potatoes. Proper deep fryers would arrive in the 20th century, but many lacked a way to control portion sizes or a sensible means of draining the old oil. In 1976, attempting to right the wrongs of existing deep fryers, Australian race car designer John Joyce ventured into a new market with his creation, the Set-n-Forget cooker. Essentially an automated deep fryer, the Set-n-Forget fried foods at temperatures up to 240 degrees F and, as its name suggests, could be left unattended without cause for concern. However, the product didn't pan out to be the hottest new item on the commercial cooking market, and it was discontinued soon after its arrival. The decades that followed would see a rise in the manufacturing of simple-yet-effective fryers featuring twin baskets and controllable oil wells. In 2000, the appliance company Waring introduced its own take on the deep fryer and soon became one of the most popular makers of the product within the food industry.

54

VEGGIE BURGER

THE VEGGIE BURGER is proof that even though some people don't eat meat, they still enjoy the culinary concept of a condiment-covered patty on a bun. Though vegetarianism has been practiced for thousands of years, the diet's signature dish is relatively young. In 1982, Gregory Sams, owner of a London-based macrobiotic restaurant called SEED, began selling a creation he called the "Vegeburger." Sams made the concoction by flavoring his homemade seitan with tamari and adding oat flakes and aduki beans to form it into a patty. The Vegeburger's success at SEED led Sams to enter the commercial market with the launch of his company Realeat, which sold packages of Vegeburger mix that consumers could rehydrate and form into a patty to cook. After a solid run as the go-to convenience food for vegetarians, the Vegeburger's time in the spotlight would be challenged by other beefless burgers that had long been in the works. In 1998, restaurant owner Paul Wenner's Gardenburger, Inc.—which sold patties made from vegetables and rice pilaf—aired an animated commercial during the *Seinfeld* finale featuring the voice of Samuel L. Jackson, which turned out to be a recipe for resounding success. Today, the veggie burger market is dominated by the likes of Boca Burger Inc., one of the most visible makers of meatless products.

55

GEORGE FOREMAN GRILL

BELIEVE IT OR NOT, the George Foreman Grill isn't the brainchild of its namesake, boxing champ George Foreman. The grill was actually invented by an Illinois man named Michael Boehm, who began promoting the grill at trade shows in the early 1990s. Though the indoor electric grill was unique in its clamshell design, it premiered to very little fanfare.

In a fortuitous turn, Boehm decided to send a sample of his invention to a marketing expert who had worked with George Foreman. At the time, Foreman was endorsing mufflers and Boehm was curious to know if he'd want to take on another product as a TV spokesperson. In an interview with CNBC in 2010, Foreman said he ignored the grill that was sent to him, admitting, "I looked at it and said, 'I'm not interested in toys.'" It wasn't until his wife Mary used it to make him a burger that Foreman was convinced to take the deal. The "George Foreman Lean Mean Fat-Reducing Grilling Machine" made its infomercial debut in 1994 and quickly became a success. Foreman's charisma and now-famous tagline, "It's so good, I put my name on it!" made the product a knockout hit with more than 100 million sold since the endorsement partnership.

SPORK

SINCE ITS INCEPTION, the spork has popped up in surprising moments throughout history. An all-in-one utensil—fork, spoon and knife—was first devised in 1874 by Samuel W. Francis, but including a knife in this culinary one-man band proved too unwieldy a proposition for the inventor. One of the first true sporks, the Göffel, was mass-produced for the German Army in World War I and included in mess kits, reducing the number of tools the soldiers had to carry around. The spork was also brought into the spotlight in 1995 during President Bill Clinton's speech at the Radio and Television Correspondents Association Dinner. The then-POTUS declared the spork the symbol of his administration, explaining, "No more false choices between the left utensil and right utensil." While Clinton's use of the unique utensil was metaphorical, the spork remains a functionally important tool in many places such as school cafeterias, campsites and prisons.

THE KEURIG

KEURIG, now synonymous with home coffee brewing, didn't initially intend for its machine to make its way into home kitchens. In the early 1990s, Keurig founder John Sylvan quit his office job in Massachusetts in order to solve a problem he was faced with daily—stale office coffee that just sat in the pot all day. His solution for fresher and better tasting coffee would be individual pods and a specialty brewer.

In 1998, the first B2000 Keurig machine and K-Cup pods were introduced for office use. Keurig began obtaining licenses for known coffee brands, eventually expanding to include other beverage options like hot chocolate and tea. Green Mountain Coffee Roasters was the first to sell their coffee in branded "K-Cups," and eventually the two companies merged in 2006 to become Keurig Green Mountain Inc. By this time, the demand for Keurigs for home use was so large that the company finally appeased their fans by releasing a smaller version for the kitchen. The home coffee brewers became the key to Keurig's success—their popularity increased sales by three times by 2014. Since then, the groggy working world has been waking up and smelling the coffee in a much more efficient—though some have argued less environmentally friendly—way.

SOUSVIDE
SUPREME

AN APPLIANCE THAT offers hands-off cooking and a high quality result pretty much sells itself. So, when the waters were tested for the SousVide Supreme in 2009, the market gave the product a warm welcome.

Sous vide, French for "under vacuum," is a cooking method that was perfected and popularized by Chef Georges Pralus in the 1970s. The technique involves placing food in airtight bags and slow-cooking them in a heated bath of water, allowing for precision temperature control within a tenth of a degree. For decades, the method would be mostly utilized in French restaurants—until Drs. Michael and Mary Dan Eades of Eades Appliance Technology found a way to bring sous vide cooking to home kitchens. Introduced in 2009, the SousVide Supreme water oven enabled not just the obvious fall-off-the-bone meats, it also welcomed a wave of creativity as home cooks began using the appliance to make the likes of pickled vegetables, puddings and infused alcohols.

On the Go

A family together at the table may be the ideal meal setting for some, but the routine hustle and bustle of life necessitates more convenient means of consumption. These objects made food the mobile entity it is today.

POTATO SACK

"My idea of heaven is a great big baked potato and someone to share it with."
—Oprah Winfrey

THROUGHOUT ITS STARCHY, steamy history, the potato has been everything from a life-saving source of nourishment for 18th and 19th century Europeans to a beloved comfort food for talk show icons. But without a sensible mode of transport, much of this crop may have stayed stuck in the dirt.

The most commonly known potato sack, the burlap bag, originated centuries ago in India,

where jute plants were used to make burlap rope, fabrics and other handwoven products. In 1855, Calcutta, India, became home to the first mill to mass produce burlap. Demand for burlap bags grew rapidly and by 1910, there were 38 burlap-producing companies exporting 450 million bags around the world. With a convenient way to carry their crops, farmers could bring larger quantities of potatoes from field to market. And the sack would prove useful beyond potatoes, famously becoming photoshoot attire for Marilyn Monroe and even being the inspiration for a unique picnic race.

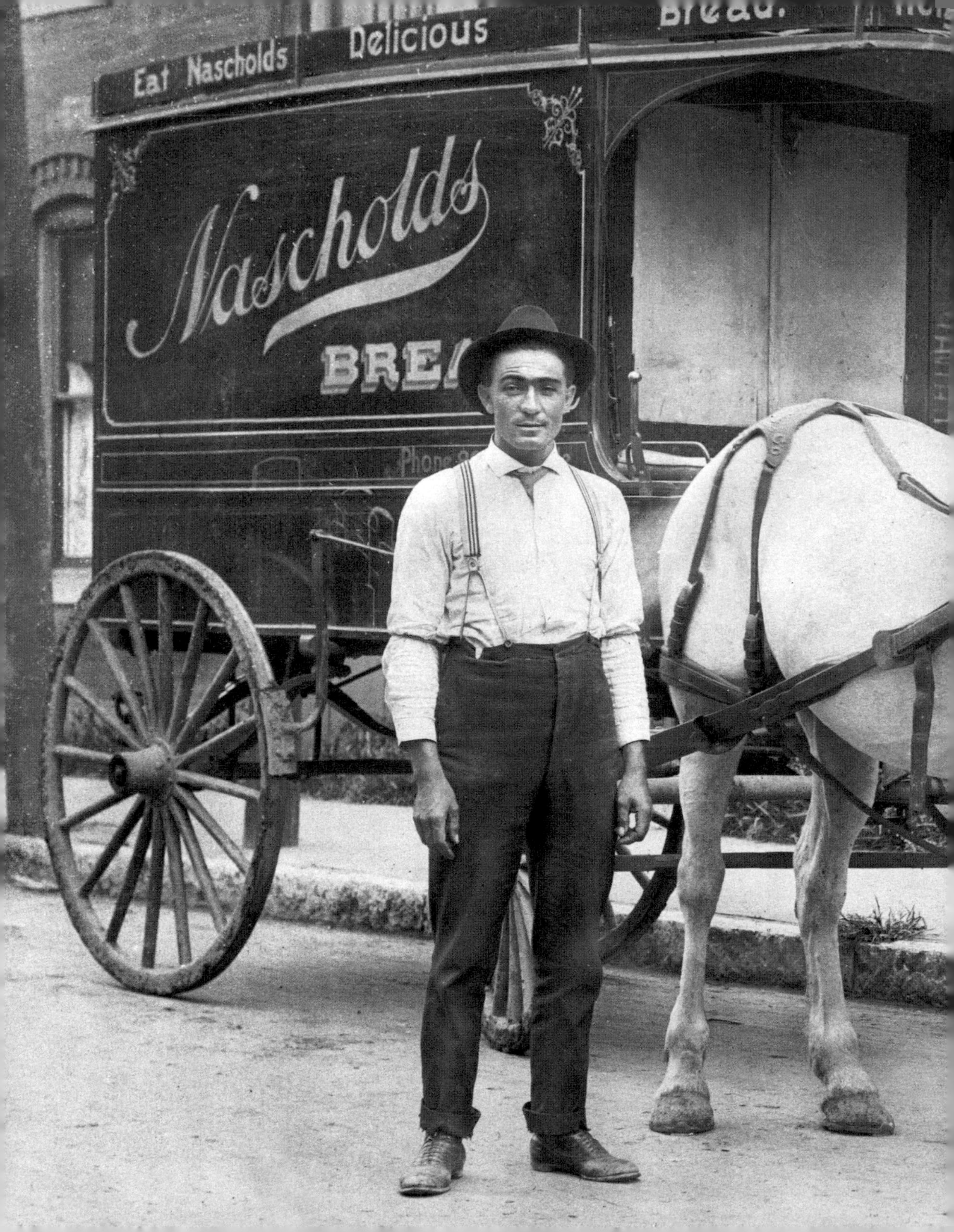
Eat Nascholds
Delicious
Nascholds

60

BAKER'S DELIVERY VAN

LONG BEFORE THE DAYS of bread loaves filling the shelves of supermarkets, bakers brought their fresh loaves straight to the front doors of their customers. And while modern bread delivery is typically done via large white vans, early baker-to-customer transactions were made possible by horse-drawn carts.

Horse-drawn bread carts were a normal sight on the streets in the 1920s, with many bakers seizing the advertising opportunity by painting their bakery names on the carts in bright, bold lettering. The smell of fresh bread coming down the street certainly didn't hurt, either, essentially serving as a scented commercial for any in the neighborhood who had yet to become part of the delivery route. And even though automobiles had already come to prominence, horse-drawn bread carts would exist all the way up to the early 1970s, paving the way for today's bread vans that keep many small bakeries in business.

61

PICNIC BASKET

PERHAPS BEST KNOWN for being Yogi Bear's perpetual object of desire, the picnic basket has been a symbol of summertime socializing for centuries. The word "picnic" is believed to come from "pique-nique," a French term from the 1600s for those who came equipped with their own wine when dining out. And until the Victorian era, the concept of a picnic was mostly only known to the wealthy.

In 1861, Isabella Beeton released an in-depth guide to Victorian-era cooking and housekeeping titled *Mrs. Beeton's Book of Household Management*, which included instructions for a proper picnic. Beeton's vision of a picnic was perhaps far more grandiose than the modern version—for a 40-person picnic, she recommends filling baskets with the likes of four roast chickens, two racks of ribs and two shoulders of lamb, three dozen biscuits, four dozen cheesecakes and many more meats, fruits, treats and beverages. The popular book brought the picnic to the mainstream, and while most middle class picnickers simplified the suggestions when filling their baskets, the concept became a timeless tradition.

62

EGG CARTON

UNLIKE THE CHICKEN and the egg, there's no debate over what came first between the egg and the carton. Eggs, a famously fragile foodstuff, have long been a prime export of farmers—but it wasn't until the early 20th century that they had a sensible mode of transportation.

In 1911, British Columbia newspaper publisher Joseph Coyle was inspired to create an egg-carrying carton after overhearing a hotelier's complaints about receiving broken eggs from a delivery man. Recognizing the opportunity, Coyle—an experimental inventor in his off time—created a carton with cushioned slots to secure each egg. Coyle made his first cartons by hand but as the demand quickly grew, he created a machine for efficient manufacturing. The success of the invention, which Coyle officially patented in 1918, allowed the former publisher to quit the newspaper business and open several egg carton factories across Canada and the U.S. And with a safe, convenient vessel, eggs became an essential item on nearly every shopper's grocery list.

63

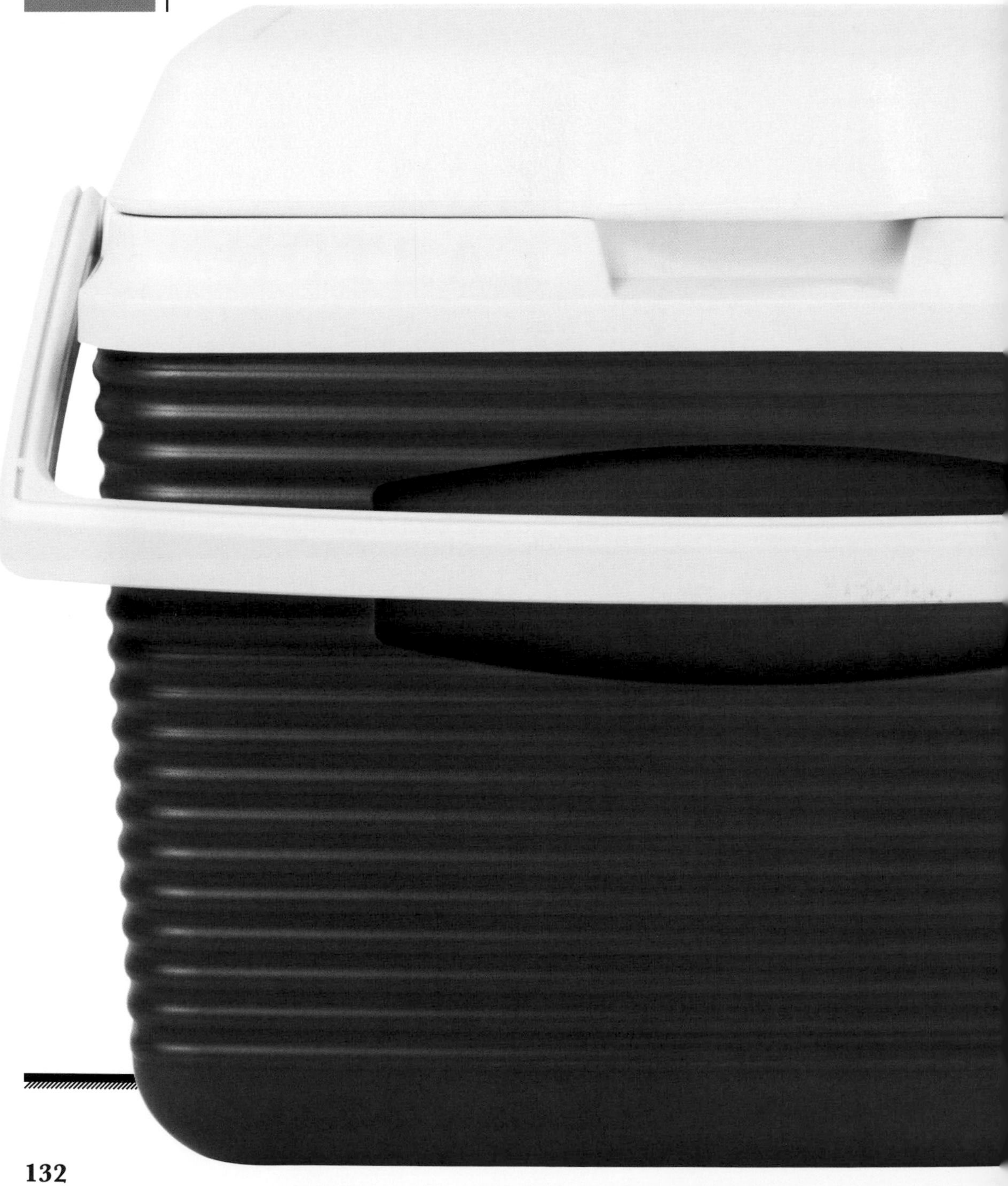

THE IGLOO COOLER

LIKE SUGAR IN lemonade or the propane in your grill, the humble cooler is an unsung hero of the American summer experience. The ability to spend all day on the hot beach with the comfort of a cold drink counts as one of life's greatest pleasures, and one made possible only through the simple—but revolutionary—item known as the cooler.

The first truly effective coolers resulted from Dow Chemical's introduction of foamed polystyrene—better known by the product name Styrofoam—to Americans in 1954, but it was Igloo's all-plastic containers (which first hit the market in 1962) that were able to combine portability, durability and effective insulation into a product still revered by beach bums and picnickers today.

64

PIZZA BOX

GENERALLY SPEAKING, cats are infinitely more interested in cardboard boxes than humans. The one exception is when the box contains a pizza pie.

The earliest pizza "boxes" were not boxes at all, instead resembling something from *Antiques Roadshow*. In the 1800s, Italian bakers would transport their pizzas and breads in a copper container called a stufa, Italian for "stove." Pizza would then emerge in America in the early 1900s, as Italian immigrants in New York and other large metropolises started selling "to-go" pies that were rolled into a cone shape, bundled in paper and tied with twine. By the 1940s, take-out pizza was both easier for consumers to find as well as easier for pizza makers to transport, with many pizzerias using grooved bases stuck in large paper bags as vessels. The following decade saw major demand for pizza to-go. Once pizza makers were forced to stack several pies as the orders piled up, the switch was made to paperboard boxes. Eventually, in the 1960s, Domino's founder Tom Monaghan commissioned Detroit-based Triad Containers to design a box specifically for pizza delivery. After careful development, the company created a box that was "simply the best," and the standard design has remained relatively unchanged ever since.

65

CHINESE TAKEOUT BOX

ICONIC AS FOLDED cardboard can possibly be, the Chinese takeout box holds an important place in America's food history. As a country that has historically prided itself on being a melting pot, diverse cultural representation is at the foundation of American cuisine. And Chinese food, through its convenience and popularity, has become a staple of takeout food in the United States.

As Chinese immigrants came to the San Francisco Bay area in the mid 1800s in hopes of capitalizing on the Gold Rush, many eventually found themselves in a variety of trades. Some decided to open restaurants, cooking the food they missed from their homeland (sweetened for the American palate)—a move that appealed to not just their fellow Chinese immigrants but also the Americans who got to try their first taste of the cuisine.

By the beginning of the 20th century, new restaurants known as "Chop Suey joints" began cropping up across metropolitan areas, largely appealing to young people. While it was later learned that chop suey was not at all a traditional Chinese dish, its popularity didn't suffer thanks to the food's affordability and take-away convenience—a cardboard box that could fold out into a plate. Today, much of the Chinese food eaten in the U.S. is Americanized, but the spirit of culture and convenience lives on just the same thanks to this unmistakable container.

Thank you

CAR CUP HOLDERS

THE THOUGHT OF driving to work without a safe place to set a cup of coffee might be downright terrifying to plenty of people today. Car cup holders, once an optional luxury, have become essential to drivers everywhere.

A 1955 Chevrolet would be one of the earliest known models to offer in-transit beverage security, as the inside of its glove compartment door featured two cup-sized indents. The '60s and '70s offered the accessory of a drink tray that could clip into the window well, but true built-in cup holders were still yet to come. In 1983, Chrysler revolutionized the convenience with the Dodge Caravan and Plymouth Voyager, which featured deep cup holders built into the dashboard plastic. But it would still be more than a decade before cup holders became universal. In 1994, McDonald's customer Stella Liebeck successfully sued the fast food company after a cup of coffee spilled on her lap in transit, causing third-degree burns. As it turned out, Liebeck's Ford Probe had no cup holders, and the infamous case fueled auto industry initiatives to implement the cup holder in all vehicles.

THE OSCAR MAYER WIENERMOBILE

THE CLASSIC HOT DOG epitomizes American comfort food, and no other brand compares to the longevity and name recognition of Oscar Mayer. For more than half a century, Americans have been melodically expressing their wish to actually be an Oscar Mayer wiener. Much of that

appeal is thanks to the iconic Wienermobile.

In 1936, Karl G. Mayer, the nephew of Oscar Mayer, saw his vision of a giant mobile hot dog manifest in the form of the original 13-foot, $5,000 Wienermobile. The vehicle would be driven all over America for decades, effectively creating a frenzy for frankfurters.

Today, Americans consume an estimated seven billion hot dogs between Memorial Day and Labor Day alone—a staggering stat that likely wouldn't exist without the decades of grassroots advertising accomplished by everyone's favorite faux frank on wheels, the Oscar Mayer Wienermobile.

MISTER SOFTEE ICE CREAM TRUCK

THE PHRASE "I scream, you scream, we all scream for ice cream" is an immortal sentiment. A refreshing taste of soft serve has been the sweet solution to summertime heat since the earlier decades of the 20th century thanks to trucks traveling through neighborhoods offering the treat to anyone within earshot. But as far as sugar-inspired siren songs go, none can compete with the alluring jingle of the Mister Softee ice cream truck.

William and James Conway, two Philadelphia brothers who realized the mass appeal of mobile ice cream trucks, decided to take their love for the creamy treat to a new

level in the 1950s. By simply bolting a soft-serve machine to the floor of a truck, they had innovated America's means of acquiring ice cream. St. Patrick's Day 1956 in West Philadelphia would be the setting of the Mister

68

Softee truck's first outing as the Conway brothers strolled the streets dishing out green ice cream to kids. While the maiden voyage wasn't particularly successful, the outings that followed were, so much so that the duo decided to franchise in 1958. The phenomenon took off far beyond Mister Softee, with myriad trucks in neighborhoods across the country serving sweet-tasting dishes of ice cream to people of all ages today.

69

SPACE FOOD TUBE

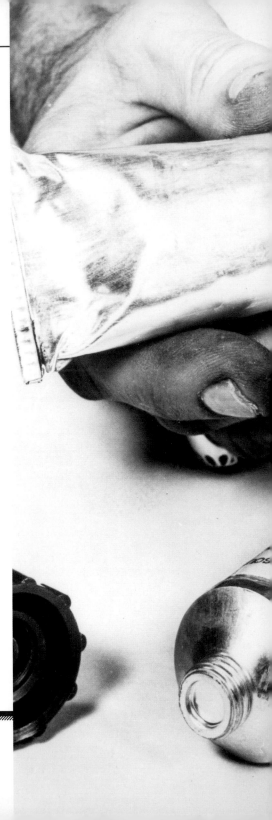

AS VAST AS IT IS, outer space isn't known for its cuisine (unless there's some misconception about what a moon pie is). So when the first astronauts set out to explore the cosmos, they had to determine how—and what—to eat in a zero gravity environment.

Aboard the *Friendship 7* spacecraft in 1962, John Glenn proved it was possible to eat in space when he consumed applesauce that had been packed in a tube. In addition to the applesauce, Glenn also received beef and vegetables in tube form prior to the flight. The nutrients were compressed into tubes so that the astronauts could easily squeeze the contents directly into their mouths. During the Gemini Program, which took place between 1962 and 1966, freeze-dried, vacuum-packed foods made their interstellar debut, setting the standard for space food efficiency, though not really moving the needle on the flavor front. A corned beef sandwich brought onboard by John Young during the Gemini 3 mission in 1965 would mark the first instance of solid food on a space flight—but sadly, the tasty upgrade crumbled in the atmosphere before it could be enjoyed.

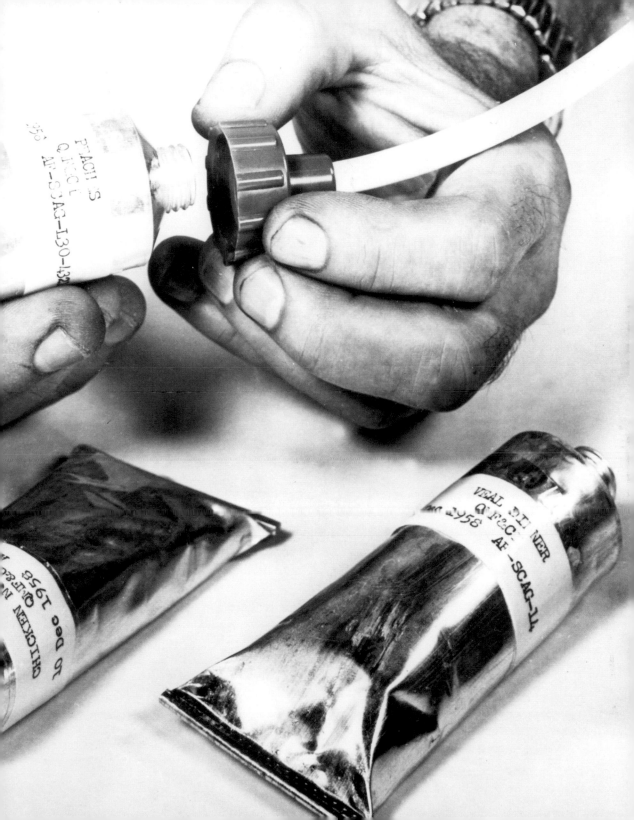

70

STARBUCKS CUP

AS ICONIC AS ANY cup of joe could ever hope to be, the Starbucks cup has become just as much a fashion accessory as it is a morning essential for the working class hero. Founded in 1971 by former University of San Francisco students Gordon Bowker, Jerry Baldwin and Zev Siegl, the Seattle-based coffee chain gradually became the go-to source of caffeine for professionals as its cafés continued to crop up across the country. As Starbucks became increasingly easy to find in metropolitan areas—with storefronts essentially being steps away from each other in some cities—the company's green mermaid-emblazoned paper cups became a multi-purpose symbol. Today, celebrities are frequently photographed clutching a cappuccino, Instagram users commonly take selfies sipping Starbucks and the world's Wall Street types are seldom seen without a cup of Pike Roast. While the consumer may vary, the Starbucks cup often sends the same message: "I'm busy."

$10 OFF

YOUR FIRST ORDER OF $15+

WHEN YOU ORDER FROM

THROUGH

seamless

USE CODE SLNYI9KDSTV2

Expires 3/31/17. Please see back for more de

71

SEAMLESS GIFT CARD

FOR YEARS, the worst part about ordering takeout over the phone was communicating with the person on the other end of the line. As impersonal as it may be, modern technology has evolved to the point where a person can make a few clicks on their computer and receive food at their front door soon after. Thanks to Seamless, you don't even have to hand the delivery guy his tip.

When the company first launched in 1999 as SeamlessWeb, their clients were strictly corporate businesses. After seven years of feeding busy bankers and lawyers, the company was acquired by Aramark in 2006—a move that yielded little success. But in 2011, after being spun off from Aramark, Seamless launched a major consumer marketing campaign to become the go-to source in cities across the country for hungry homebodies and professionals looking to get a meal without uttering a word or reaching for their wallet. The move paid off—in 2013 alone, after merging with Grubhub, the company generated more than $100 million in revenue. And the Seamless gift card has become the perfect accompaniment to a birthday card, because who doesn't want to order free food from the comfort of their couch?

Restaurant Culture

As humanity began adopting more elaborate rituals, the act of eating evolved from primal practice to social opportunity. Businesses soon capitalized on the shift, and the dining experience was forever changed.

72

TOQUE (CHEF'S HAT)

IT MAY NOT be the most fashionable hat to stroll down the street in, but the traditional toque is a longstanding symbol of culinary expertise. Around 300 A.D. when Greece was invaded by the Byzantine Empire, many chefs seeking safety fled to monasteries and began wearing tall stovepipe hats to fit in with the monks. Even after the fallout, some continued to wear the hats in solidarity. Millennia later, French chefs adopted a similar look for their own uniforms, dubbing their tall hats "toques," possibly borrowing the Arabic term for "hat."

In 1815, white became the official color of toques when the personal chef of French prime minister Charles Maurice de Talleyrand suggested it was the most hygienic color. And the pleats, while sometimes a mere matter of aesthetic appeal added to the otherwise cylindrical hats, have been known to represent the number of ways the chef can cook his or her specialty. While toques have fallen to the wayside for many modern gourmet chefs as restaurant culture evolves, they remain one of the most iconic pieces of food industry history.

WINE GLASS

A BYOW POLICY—especially one with a minimal corkage fee—is always a smart way for any restaurant to get a steady stream of diners in the door. But while customers may love being able to bring their own wine when they dine out, few are likely to take their most precious stemware from the safety of its cabinet. Wine glasses, in their many incarnations throughout history, have always been a means of displaying social status. In the Roman Empire, the upper class would drink their wine from silver and clay pottery goblets. During the Middle Ages, silver bowls were used in social gatherings to scoop wine for tasting purposes as well as to prove the liquid wasn't poison (a common concern at the time). The 1300s were somewhat of an experimental phase for wine vessels, with one of the most common forms being a pitcher made of leather known as a black jack. In the late 1700s, the closest incarnation to the modern wine glass was created when each of London's Freemason Lodges began using fine jacobite glasses, which consisted of a small goblet and a long stem. More than a century later in the late 1950s, the Austrian glassware company Riedel began creating what is still considered to be one of the finest wine glasses in the world.

THE SOUFFLÉ

SOUFFLÉ IS A CLASSIC FRENCH DISH known for its delicacy and difficulty. At its most basic, soufflé is a dish of egg yolks and whipped egg whites folded into a béchamel, then baked until perfectly puffed with a saucy center, as its name implies—the word soufflé comes from the French verb souffler, which means "to blow."

While the basic principles of a soufflé are simple, perfecting a soufflé requires careful timing and a practiced hand. So many things can go wrong: Overbeaten egg whites will fall apart with the addition of other ingredients; overcooking will yield a dry soufflé; baking the soufflé on the top rack of the oven will cause it to brown too quickly.

Soufflés are also famed in pop culture history as a plot device to evoke disappointment: When the souffle falls, so do the chef's spirits. However, this expects too much from a soufflé; even the best ones only retain their shape for three to four minutes before falling.

75

CHILDREN'S MENU

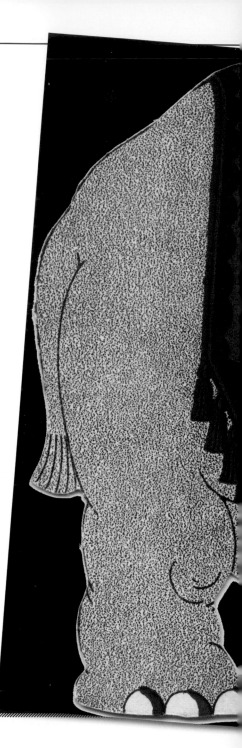

WHILE PROHIBITION—which took effect in January 1920—was a source of frustration for many adults in the U.S., the period was actually a bit of a renaissance for hungry kids. Without alcohol sales to rely on, the restaurant industry found itself needing a new market to tap in order to survive. At the time, most restaurants had policies against serving children unless they were guests at adjacent hotels—or they did until the Waldorf Astoria in New York boldly decided to create a menu specifically for children in 1921. Printed on pink paper featuring the nursery rhyme character Little Jack Horner, the Waldorf-Astoria's kid-exclusive menu had a similar fun feel to those of today. The offerings, however, were far from the chicken nuggets and grilled cheeses offered now. Dishes such as broiled lamb chops were standard fare for kiddie diners at the Waldorf Astoria as well as the restaurant at Marshall Field's department store in Chicago, who also adopted the children's menu trend at the time. Fortunately for the youth of America, the industry eventually decided to give kids what they want on their menus. A bag of crayons and a paper placemat was a wise move, too.

MENU for CHILDREN

Tea Rooms, Seventh Floor

MARSHALL FIELD & COMPANY

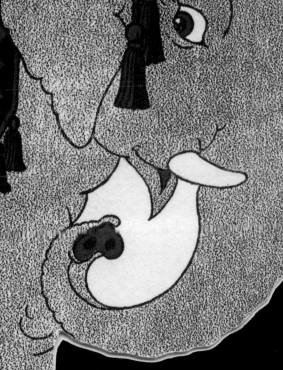

TRAY

WHETHER IT'S BEING used to carry meals in a school cafeteria, a prison dining hall or a buffet line, the fiberglass tray is often associated with less-than-stellar cuisine. Nonetheless, its introduction marks an important moment in restaurant history. After experiencing the concept of a smörgåsbord in Sweden, John Kruger introduced his own version at the Chicago World's Fair in 1893. Kruger called his Americanized smörgåsbord a "cafeteria," a Spanish term for "coffee shop." William and Samuel Childs, with their chain of Childs Restaurants originating in New York City, would add their own innovation to the cafeteria and buffet concept by introducing tray lines to their self service restaurants in the 1920s. The popularity of self-service dining, complete with trays, would take off quickly as Childs Restaurants expanded far beyond New York and opened more than 120 restaurants across the country. With its apparent convenience and efficiency, the style of food service was soon applied to a wide variety of institutions—none of which have been able to solve the "every tray is wet" scenario that arises from stacking them after a good wash.

MCDONALD'S GOLDEN ARCHES

TO THE AVERAGE CITIZEN of the world, a giant, vibrant "M" towering in the distance is an unmistakable sight. Available in 119 countries today, McDonald's is familiar fare to people of all walks of life, and much of that familiarity stems from its iconic signage.

In 1952, brothers Richard and Maurice McDonald were seeking architects to construct their first restaurant, which would feature two semicircular arches on each side of the building. Architect Stanley Clark Meston would bring the vision to life, and the unique design of the McDonald's restaurant quickly became famous. While the arches were not initially intended to resemble the letter, the company capitalized on the building's fame and created a logo featuring the arches united to form an "M." By the '60s, the architectural arches were retired and the golden arches logo had become a permanent fixture. Instantly recognizable, the sign means the same thing today as it did decades ago: a satiating solution to your super sized hunger is just minutes away.

78

FOUNTAIN SODA GLASS

WHILE THEY MAY not be considered health hubs today, soda fountains were created to replicate the bubbly natural mineral waters used in ancient civilizations for varying medicinal purposes. The first to recreate this natural health source was Joseph Priestley in 1767, who discovered that infusing carbon dioxide into water would recreate the fizziness. Johann Schweppe—whose name can still be found on soda cans today—then began adding flavors to mineral water in 1783. Instead of sugar, he infused salts to mimic mineral waters from springs around the world. By the 19th century, chemists were experimenting with better-selling flavors, easier dispension and refrigeration improvements. The biggest name in soda innovation was John Matthews, who helped form the American Soda Fountain Company in 1891. Soda fountains then became a staple in pharmacies, candy stores and ice cream parlors, helmed by "soda jerks," who got their moniker from the job's task of swinging the handle when adding soda water. In the 1950s, when drive-ins and fast-food chains were becoming the norm in American suburbia, soda fountains went from being the sole attraction of an establishment to an important asset. The soda fountains of today—some of which are equipped with touch-screen technology—remain as vital as ever to anyone looking to fill a glass or paper cup with soda, a root beer float or any other variation of satisfying, sugary carbonation.

79

THE LOBSTER BIB

IN 17TH CENTURY EUROPE, people were expected to bring their own bibs when they were invited to dine at a nobleman's house. Dressed their best, they tied napkins around their necks before eating to protect their clothing from spills. The phrase "trouble making ends meet" was attributed to men failing to properly tie their napkins around their neck—a symbol of not having enough status to dine with noblemen.

But one thing these bib-wearing members of high society never ate was lobster. The crustacean was actually so abundant that eating one was a sign of poverty—a food reserved for house pets and prisoners. Lobster's lowbrow status remained until the late 19th century when socialites from landlocked cities began vacationing to Maine for the "exotic" seafood, which included fresh-boiled lobster. By the 1900s, the demand for lobster had grown so much that fisherman could not catch enough to keep up, leading to a surge in prices. Often reserved for posh weddings and Hollywood parties, the newly respected dish led to the reintroduction of bibs for the same reason they were used in the 17th century—to protect high society from spills during special events.

Cultural
Icons

While some foods and their associated objects have only ever served the purpose of sustenance or culinary convenience, others have managed to capture the zeitgeist.

80

WEDDING CAKE TOPPER

AS FAR AS FOODS GO, cake is a timeless signifier of celebration. People eat it to usher in another year of their lives or to celebrate a professional accomplishment. But most significantly, people shell out copious amounts of cash on cakes to commemorate tying the knot.

The wedding cake can be traced all the way back to the Roman Empire. While the Romans' cakes lacked the grandeur of modern matrimonial masterpieces, they were still a focal point of the post-wedding celebration. By the time of the Victorian era, white wedding cakes became the tradition, as it was believed that the color represented the bride's purity.

While its exact origins are unknown, an anecdotal legend suggests the first bride and groom figurine topper was created by a baker whose daughter was getting married. Determined to adorn the cake with a unique symbol of love, as his daughter requested, the baker created two figurines resembling his daughter and her groom-to-be. Since then, the tradition of the cake topper has stuck, evolving with the times to now include groom-and-groom and bride-and-bride incarnations.

PAUL CÉZANNE'S KITCHEN TABLE (STILL LIFE WITH BASKET)

IN THE EARLY ERAS of human history, food was seldom seen as more than a mere necessity for survival. But as society evolved, the perception of food began to blossom into something greater, with the focus often on the aesthetics as much as the flavor. Works such as Cézanne's *Kitchen Table (Still-Life with basket)* show that a large of part of that shift in perception is owed to the art world.

In the 19th century, French painter Paul Cézanne set out to explore the forms of everyday objects by painting still-life portraits. His muse, most frequently, was fruit. "I shall astonish Paris with an apple," the painter once famously said. While his work was initially met with harsh criticism from many in the artistic community, it would later inspire generations of art teachers and students to follow in his footsteps. And the perception of food as art has far from ceased, with entire galleries today showcasing delicious-looking subjects and chefs everywhere devoting serious attention to plate presentation.

WHITE HOUSE STATE DINNER MENU

LARGE RECEPTIONS were rare in Washington until the White House underwent renovations in 1902. With a new and improved interior, the presidential palace could now better reflect America's global status as the commander in chief welcomed visiting heads of state and other dignitaries. State dinners became a common event from that point on, with the receptions organized by the first lady and her staff, who influence everything from the guest list to the entertainment. But as important as the attendees are, the most crucial part of a state dinner is the menu, which takes special care to reflect the national cuisine of the head of state visiting. Traditionally five courses, the meal is typically planned and prepared by the White House Executive Chef, who uses local ingredients and American influences to honor the guest's culture. An exception to this was during President Obama's last State Dinner in October 2016 where he hosted Italian Prime Minister Matteo Renzi and his wife Agnese Landini. The food was prepared by celebrity chef Mario Batali, whose menu included pesto appetizers, agnolotti pasta, squash salad, crostata and traditional fruits from Italy. What better venue to host one of the world's most renowned chefs than the White House?

DINNER

Cold Columbia River Salmon en Bellevue
Schloss Johannisberg 1969   Sauce Verte
    Paillettes Dorées

Roast Sirloin of Beef Bordelaise
Louis Martini Cabernet Sauvignon 1968   Mushrooms Provençale
   Artichokes St. Germain

Bibb Lettuce Salad
Brie Cheese
Louis Roederer Cristal 1967

Mousse au Chocolat

THE WHITE HOUSE
Friday, August 16, 1974

LEMONADE STAND

AMERICAN CHILDREN HAVE been making their summertime salary with lemonade since the 19th century. The earliest stand was rumored to have been started by 10-year-old Edward Bok—who after immigrating to Brooklyn from the Netherlands, was looking to help support his family in any way he could. In 1873, he began selling ice water on road sides for 1 cent. When other kids began copying him, he started squeezing lemon into the water and upped the price to 3 cents a cup. By 1880, *The New York Times* reported that children all over New York City were setting up stands to make money, which quickly spread across the country. The entrepreneurial skills Bok earned as the first lemonade sales kid paid off—he later went on to pioneer the advice column in *Ladies Home Journal*, coined the term "living room" and introduced America to a trendy new living module called the bungalow. After reading his autobiography *A Dutch Boy Fifty Years After*, President Franklin D. Roosevelt said of Bok, "He is the only man I ever heard of who changed, for the better, the architecture of an entire nation, and he did it so quickly and yet so effectively that we didn't know it was begun before it was finished." And it began with a lemonade stand.

FROSTED FLAKES BOX

IN 1894, BROTHERS Dr. John Kellogg and W.K. Kellogg were running the Battle Creek Sanitarium in Michigan. Many of their health practices derived from John's strict Adventist beliefs—one of them being that flavorful food led people to sin. On a religious pursuit to create new bland foods, John accidentally invented "corn flakes" in 1898. Frustrated by his brother's stubbornness to keep his cereal unsweetened, W.K. bought the rights to manufacture the flakes, changed the recipe, and started the Kellogg Company in 1906.

Although the corn flakes were successful, they wouldn't become the bestselling breakfast cereal until the 1950s, when advertising agency Leo Burnett was hired to create a marketing campaign for the newly named "Sugar Frosted Flakes." To appeal to kids, the company created four potential characters for the cereal box: Katy the Kangaroo, Newt the Gnu, Elmo the Elephant and Tony the Tiger. Tony instantly won everyone over and was selected over the other animals. Voiced by Thurl Ravenscroft and featured on TV and radio shows, Tony's popularity led Kellogg's to transform the beloved mascot into a fully upright character with a backstory. During the 1970s, he was given an Italian-American nationality and a family—Mama Tony, Mrs. Tony, Antoinette and Tony Jr. The marketing success of Tony was so "grrrreat," children's cereals eventually became synonymous with memorable mascots including Toucan Sam, Lucky the Leprechaun and the Trix Rabbit.

85

RUSSELL STOVER'S CHOCOLATE BOX

"My mama always said life was like a box of chocolates—you never know what you're gonna get."
—*Forrest Gump*

A NAME NOW synonymous with boxed chocolates, Russell Stover first entered the confectionery world by way of ice cream. After working for various candy companies and manufacturers, Stover partnered with Christian Nelson in 1921 to create the first chocolate dipped ice cream bar, the Eskimo Pie. Though the treat was a huge success, Stover left the business in 1923 to partner with someone closer to him—his wife Clara Stover. After moving to Denver, Clara began making hand dipped chocolates in the couple's new kitchen. The carefully crafted chocolates were sold in their now iconic boxes and "Mrs. Stover's Bungalow Candies" quickly gained recognition throughout the city—by 1925, the Stovers had already opened seven stores and two chocolate factories. By the time Russell died in 1954, the company that had recently taken his namesake had grown to produce 11 million pounds of candy a year. Russell Stover's candies would later influence one of the most memorable lines in cinema history, and the chocolates still remain a vital treat on Valentine's Day.

86

TV DINNERS

THE TALE OF the TV dinner is often traced back to a Swanson salesman named Gerry Thomas. In the fall of 1953, food company C.A. Swanson &

Sons overestimated the popularity of their Thanksgiving turkey. Left with 260 tons of unsold turkey, they challenged their employees to come up with a way to solve their excess bird problem. Thomas suggested they use single compartment foil trays used on airplanes to house a fully prepared and frozen Thanksgiving dinner.

While smaller brands had attempted to sell

frozen dinners, it was Swanson's marketing that made them a success. In 1953, 20 million households in America had a TV, and families were hooked on evening programs such as *I Love Lucy*, *Dragnet* and *The Milton Berle Show*. Swanson hopped on the new TV craze and used the name "TV Dinner" to brand their product. The trays were packaged in a box designed to look like a television, and the association

between nightly TV watching and frozen dinners took off. The pre-made meals also meant moms could spend more time pursuing hobbies or careers instead of being confined to the kitchen. The first TV dinners were sold for about $1 and included cornbread stuffing, peas, sweet potatoes and turkey. By the end of their first year in production, Swanson had sold 10 million TV dinners.

WALT DISNEY'S "LADY AND THE TRAMP"
FIRST ALL CARTOON FEATURE IN CINEMASCOPE
In Color by Technicolor

WALT DISNEY'S "LADY AND THE TRAMP"
FIRST ALL CARTOON FEATURE IN CINEMASCOPE
In Color by Technicolor

87

LADY AND THE TRAMP LOBBY CARDS

IN 1955, two cartoon canines proved the romantic potential of pasta. Italian restaurants have long been a popular date spot, but the Walt Disney animated feature *Lady and the Tramp* would make the world see spaghetti and meatballs in a whole new way as its characters, the lavish-living Lady and the independent mutt Tramp, share a long noodle that results in an accidental kiss. The scene became iconic, leading to numerous animated parodies from the likes of the TV series *Family Guy*, *The Simpsons* and even Disney's own *Kronk's New Groove* in 2005. Even the animated meal itself got the tribute treatment when *Cooking Light* magazine published a recipe for "*Lady and the Tramp* Spaghetti and Meatballs" in 1998.

EGGO WAFFLES

**"A waffle is like a pancake with
a syrup trap."**

—Mitch Hedberg

COMBINING GEOMETRIC ingenuity
with culinary expertise, waffles have long
been a day-starting staple. But no waffle has
ever achieved the notoriety of the frozen,
yellow-boxed variety perfected by Eggo.

After seeing success selling mayonnaise,
brothers Frank, Sam and Anthony Dorsa
of San Jose, California, decided to expand
their Eggo company to include waffle mix.
With frozen food was on the rise and a
limited geographic reach of fresh batter,
the brothers needed a means of mass-
producing premade waffles. In 1953, Frank
Dorsa found the solution by inventing a
contraption powered by a merry-go-round
engine that controlled several waffle irons at
once. Eggo waffles would be a hit at diners
in the years that followed until Kellogg
bought the brand in the 1970s and launched
them into the mainstream. In 1972, the
slogan "Leggo my Eggo" made its mark on
the pop culture lexicon for decades to come.
The phrase was briefly retired between 2009
and 2014, but it would take on a new life in
2016. In a scene from the hit Netflix series
Stranger Things, the psychokinetic Eleven
reveals her obsession for Eggo waffles by
stealing several boxes from a grocery store
and shattering the automatic door with her
mind on the way out.

TWINKIE

NOTHING QUITE EPITOMIZES the advent of processed, pre-packaged snack foods like the Twinkie. Between urban myths of near-immortality ("They never expire!") and the nostalgic allure of cream-filled sponge cake, Twinkies have held our fascination for decades. They were even selected to be preserved in the National Millennium Time Capsule (though, unfortunately, they've since been removed to assuage worries that their presence would attract mice).

When they were invented on April 6, 1930, Hostess Twinkies were baked with a banana filling. As bananas became scarce due to World War II rations, Hostess switched to the vanilla filling we're familiar with today. While this change was clearly popular, Twinkies didn't become truly iconic until the '50s, when Hostess sponsored *The Howdy Doody Show* and included a cowboy character named "Twinkie the Kid."

The Twinkie's now-infamous reputation for longevity was popularized in the '60s; Americans who feared nuclear attacks notoriously stocked their bomb shelters with the snack cake. Yet despite assertions from a retired science teacher in Maine that a Twinkie kept on top of his blackboard for 30 years was brittle but "probably still edible," Twinkie manufacturers state the shelf-life is only 45 days (still slightly longer than the shelf-life of 26 days they were originally listed as having).

Nonetheless, Twinkies are undeniably resilient. While they may not survive a nuclear attack, they did survive a bankruptcy. When Hostess operations shut down in November 2012, the absence of Twinkies didn't last long. Apollo Global Management and Metropoulos & Co. purchased Twinkies (and other famous Hostess treats), and they returned to shelves in July 2013.

PILLSBURY DOUGHBOY

REFRIGERATED DOUGH MAY NOT seem like the kind of thing that would require a mascot, but it's hard to imagine a world without the portly little baker known as the Pillsbury Doughboy. Founded in Minneapolis, Minnesota, by Charles Pillsbury in 1872, Pillsbury has long been a household name for anyone looking for an easy means of making everything from dinner rolls to Christmas

cookies. And much of that fame is thanks to an advertising campaign that began in 1965. After creating a successful jingle for the company, the Chicago-based Leo Burnett ad agency created the Pillsbury Doughboy to be featured in commercials. The Doughboy was given the name Poppin' Fresh by Rudy Perez, a copywriter at the agency, as an attempt to tout the freshness of Pillsbury products. But the name didn't turn out to have the same staying power as the character's cry of "hoo hoo!" each time he's poked in the tummy. Pillsbury has experimented with several products that turned out to be not so hot in recent decades, though they've yet to abandon the beloved mascot. Since his debut in 1965, the Pillsbury Doughboy has appeared in more than 600 commercials for the company.

NET WT 8 OZ (226g)

PER ROLL

100 CALORIES

2g SAT FAT

210mg SODIUM

3g SUGARS

91

SPAM

CHOPPED PORK AND HAM

SPAM

CANNED, PRECOOKED MEAT may not sound appetizing to those unfamiliar with this iconic product. But to many, SPAM is an important milestone in the history of American home cooking.

Hormel Foods Corporation first introduced their concoction—which is mostly comprised of pork shoulder and ham—in 1937. The meaty product's first true wave of popularity first came during World War II, though, as its convenience and availability made it the perfect choice for the U.S. to feed soldiers abroad. From there, SPAM began spreading across the rest of the world, becoming a staple for school lunches and a simple solution for family meals at home.

A polarizing pork product if there ever were one, SPAM is celebrated today by those who truly love its taste as well as those who claim to enjoy it ironically. Between novelty T-shirts, homemade Etsy products and a Monty Python sketch, today's culture is steadfast in continuing the legacy of Hormel's famous creation.

92

SLIM-FAST CAN

AMERICA HAS ALWAYS BEEN a land of plenty, but as our waistlines have expanded over the past few decades, so has our appetite for new products to help us shed unwanted weight. In 1977, there was a new addition to our arsenal in the Battle of the Bulge a drink called Slim-Fast.

Originally marketed as a meal-replacement milkshake by Thompson Medical, the success of the Slim-Fast beverage (which provides around 200 calories per can) propelled its rise to cultural ubiquity during the late '80s and '90s. Celebrities such as Whoopi Goldberg and Kathie Lee Gifford threw their support behind the product, which eventually evolved to encompass a line of snacks and pre-packaged meals to provide customers with a complete dietary plan for torching fat. Today, with people still struggling to become their best selves, Slim-Fast continues to succeed.

What's my bag?
It's milk, baby, yeah!

The calcium in lowfat or fat free milk helps to prevent osteoporosis and keep my bones strong. So I can keep my mojo working overtime. Oh, *behave.*

got milk?

93

GOT MILK? AD

FEW PHOTOS can elicit '90s nostalgia quite like a smirking, milk-mustachioed Patrick Ewing. Or a milk-mustachioed Vanna White. Or Jonathan Taylor Thomas (with or without the milk 'stache). Supported by an undisputedly strong celebrity cast, the Got Milk? campaign was created by the Goodby, Silverstein & Partners ad firm in 1993 and brought to the mainstream by the Milk Processor Education Program. Seeking ways to revive declining milk consumption, the national marketing campaign perfected the art of mass appeal right out of the gate by featuring some of the most famous names of the era proudly sporting streaks of dairy on their upper lip. For the remainder of the decade and well into the new millennium, Got Milk? ads would appear in everything from magazines to high school cafeterias, appealing to consumers through the likes of athletes, musicians, movie stars and even beloved cartoon characters. The slogan was retired in 2014 and replaced with "Milk Life," a line aimed to push the protein benefits of the beverage.

Novelty
Items

While food itself is essential, its many manifestations are not. Over time, our love for the things we eat has resulted in many unique—and at times, questionable—creations.

94

BUTTER SCULPTURE

AS FUN AS macaroni jewelry or making a ketchup smiley face on a burger may be, nothing in the culinary world quite compares to the artistic quality of butter. In 1876, the first famous American butter sculpture would make its debut at the Centennial Exhibition in Philadelphia, Pennsylvania. Sculpted by Arkansas dairy farmer Caroline Shawk Brooks, the work—a bas-relief titled *Dreaming Iolanthe*, which featured the face of the heroine from the play *King René's Daughter*—had to be preserved over a bucket of ice that was frequently being refilled. The piece was widely acclaimed, even receiving praise in *The New York Times*, and numerous other butter sculptors would emerge soon after. At the 1904 St. Louis Louisiana Purchase Exposition, sculpted butter was booming as artists showed off massive works such as a 600-pound statue of a milkmaid milking a cow. Refrigeration advancements in the early 20th century would take butter-sculpting to entirely new levels as the art form's popularity continued to spread across the country. At any given state fair today, you're likely to find a display room of salty, pale-yellow masterpieces.

95

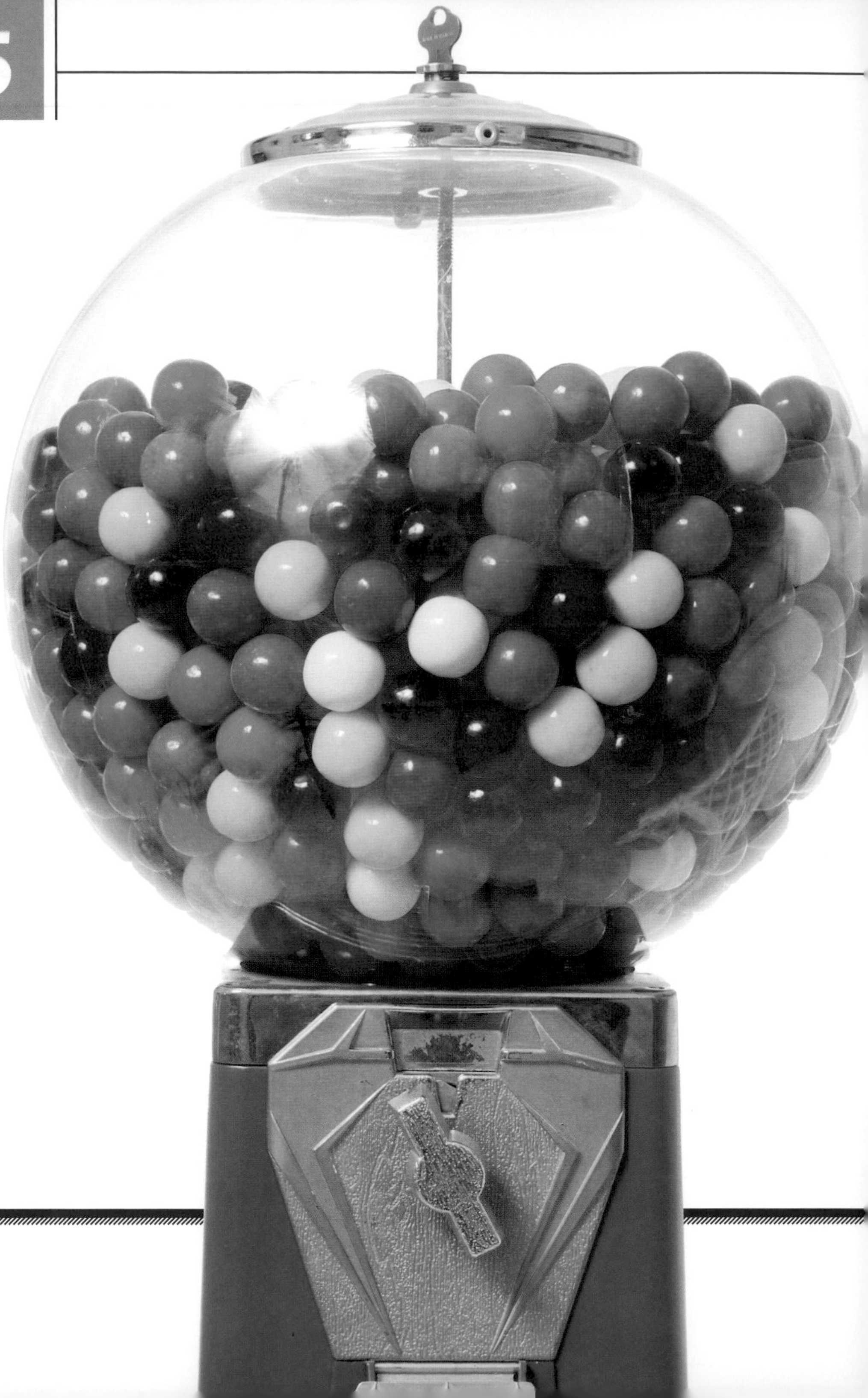

GUMBALL MACHINE

THE STORY SURROUNDING the gumball's origin may be as sugarcoated as the chewable sphere itself. In the early 1900s, a German grocer in New York—whose name was not recorded for posterity—became frustrated with the poor sales of his chewing gum and threw a wadded piece across the store. The gum landed in a sugar barrel, which gave it an appealing, glistening appearance. Looking to present the sugary-covered gum in a new way, the grocer modified a peanut vending machine so that it could dispense the pieces. Thomas Adams Gum Company, which had already been selling stick gum in vending machines, then introduced the first proper gumball machine in 1907, though the gumballs of the time were not yet the colorful kind known today. That aspect would not come until 1928, when accountant Walter Diemer invented a gum with enough elasticity to blow bubbles, which he colored pink due to it being the only food coloring hue he had on hand. Diemer's bubble gum, called Dubble Bubble, was then sold in colorful gumball form in machines across the country—a trend that has carried on ever since.

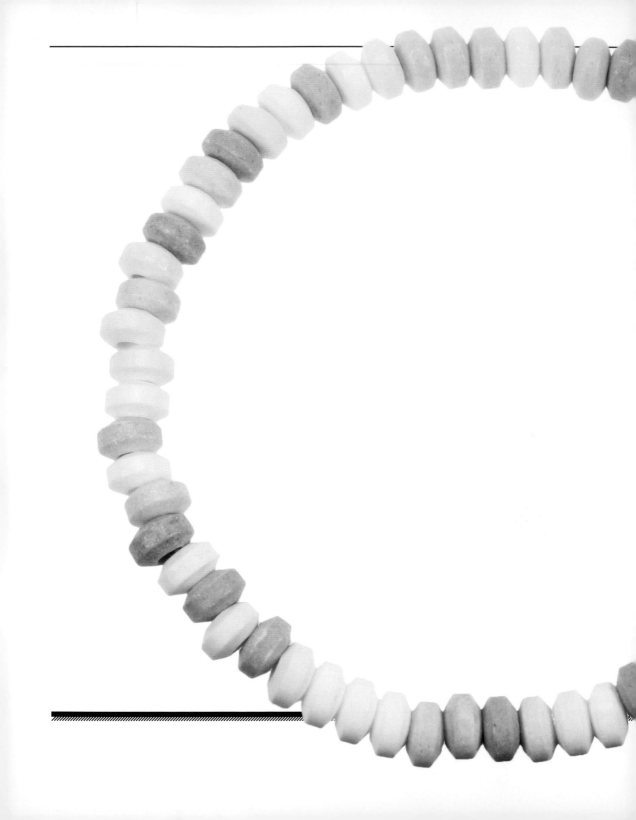

CANDY NECKLACE

OFTEN ONE OF THE first pieces of jewelry given to any child in America, the candy necklace has been serving as the centerpiece of edible fashion for more than half a century.

First introduced by the Smarties company in 1958, the candy necklace was an exciting development for fans of the vibrant candy pieces the creators were known for. Candy necklaces fit for the average neck were plenty popular in the decades that followed, though that didn't stop Koko's Confectionery & Novelty from setting out to stretch the sugary jewelry's possibilities. On December 17, 2014, the candy creators made the wildest dreams of sweet-toothed children come true when they unveiled a 5,361-foot confection that set a Guinness World Record for Longest Candy Necklace.

BURGER KING CROWN

FAST FOOD HAS BEEN analyzed and criticized tirelessly in recent years, but thanks to the industry's advertising, its appeal remains unyielding. Burger King may not be the top juggernaut of deep-fried efficiency, but its simple, straightforward iconography is nothing short of well-done. While the burger company has revamped its image and subsequent ads numerous times since its founding in 1954, the Burger King "crown" has remained consistent.

The 1970s saw Burger King take the obvious advertising route with its name, revealing animated versions of a magical man representing beef royalty in an effort to sway the appetites of children. After phasing out the cartoon kings, the fast-food chain attempted to attract a larger audience in the early 2000s with a human mascot dressed as a caricatured king. However, due to widespread ridicule on the internet and an overall consensus that the new "King" was inherently "creepy," Burger King semi-retired the character in 2011.

Throughout its search for a fitting royal icon to represent its brand, Burger King has succeeded with the simple act of providing paper crowns to the children who eat at their restaurants. The thrill of a mock coronation for their birthday party, preschool graduation or any other occasion continues to bring burger-hungry kids and their families to Burger King franchises today.

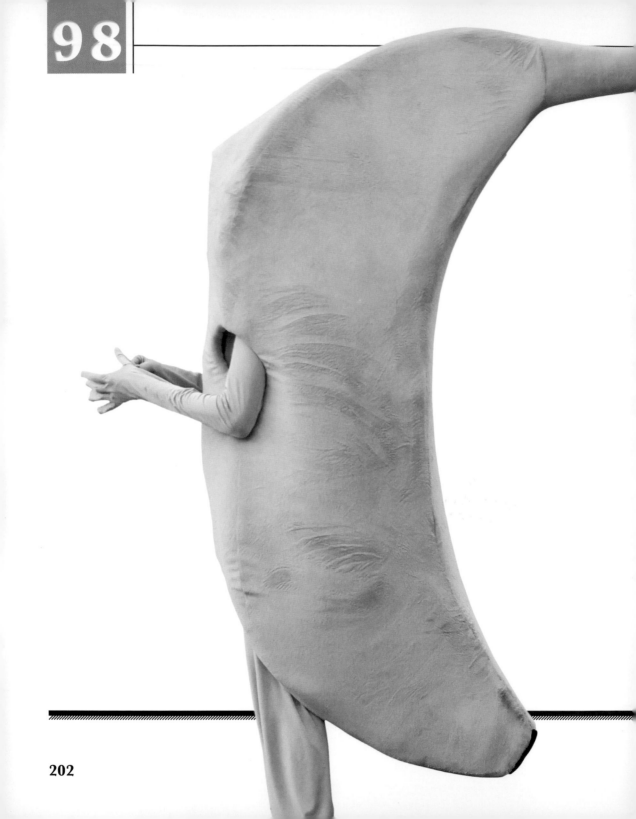

98

BANANA COSTUME

FEW FOODS IN history have proven as fruitfully funny as the banana. In 1917, the banana would reveal its slapstick value, causing a waiter to slip and spill a tray of food in the silent film *The Flirt*. The slippery banana peel would become a comedy trope in the decades after, but the banana itself continued to be ripe for new gags. In 1992, children would be treated to the sight of grown adults dressed in banana costumes in the Australian TV series *Bananas in Pyjamas*. Complete with its catchy theme song, the series would come to America soon after, yielding numerous unique collectibles such as banana plush toys modeled after the characters. The banana costume's appeal would not be exclusive to children, however. While filming a low-budget TV show in 2005, a man dressed in a banana costume, dubbed "Banana Boy," was arrested for a staged fight with his friends in Glens Falls, New York. And today, bunches of banana costumes can be found in every costume store.

99

BACŌN COLOGNE

BACON HAS OFTEN been placed in a class of its own. Between its crispy texture, salty flavor and greasy goodness, the pork product's appeal is easy to see, but it's the smell—that savory smell capable of trasnporting us to kitchens long forgotten—that might be the true secret to its success.

In 2011, cologne company Fargginay unveiled a scent that promised to be a sizzling-hot item in the fragrance world. The brand's Bacōn cologne (pronounced "bay-cone") was inspired by its namesake, Parisian butcher John Fargginay, who in 1920 began mixing essential oils with the essence of bacon to produce an alluring aroma for his customers. Modernizing the idea, the Fargginay company decided to contain their cologne in sleek bottles featuring a strip of bacon resembling the figure of a voluptuous woman, with the slogan "scent by the gods." And for just $36, who wouldn't want to smell like sexualized breakfast food?

bacōn®

by fargginay

scent by the gods

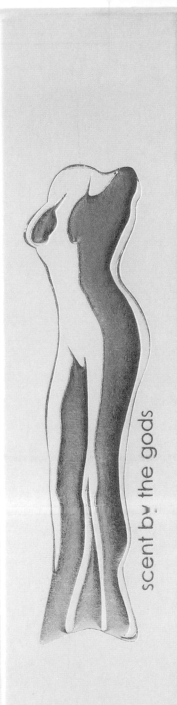

scent by the gods

SCENTED BILLBOARD

THROUGHOUT ITS JUICY HISTORY, steak hasn't had much trouble appealing to the masses. But in 2010, the Bloom grocery store in North Carolina believed quality photos of sizzling steak simply weren't cutting it as an effective means of marketing anymore and decided to go the extra mile. The company chose 1220 River Highway just outside of Catawba County as the home for its unusual yet undeniably innovative new marketing method: A scented billboard. Featuring a giant fork hoisting a 3-D slice of steak and a french fry on the end, the billboard aimed to promote Bloom's new beef brand, Sheffield & Sons, by emitting scents scheduled for the hours of 7 to 10 a.m. and 4 to 7 p.m. each day. The billboard was one of the first of its kind and demonstrated that food marketing need not be limited to just a few of the five senses.

IPHONE BOWL

ONCE A NOTORIOUSLY lonely act, dining at a table for one became much more manageable for many people across the globe following the advent of the iPhone. With the ability to peruse the internet while slurping a sporkful of noodles, convenience and comfort seemed to be at an all-time high. But as it goes in the tech world—and the food world— there's always room for further innovation.

In 2013, design firm MisoSoupDesign introduced a product aiming to make the joys of eating and iPhoning not just more convenient, but also cuisine-specific. Given an exceptionally self-aware name, the Anti-Loneliness Ramen Bowl is crafted with a slot that serves as a smartphone holder so users can enjoy hands-free phone entertainment as they chow down on instant ramen. Of course, the bowl practically necessitates investing in a screen cover to shield your phone from splashes of spicy broth, but the soup selfie benefits outweigh the cost.